NINE RUBIES

by Mahru Ghashghaei

as told to Susan Snyder

ISBN: 978-1-930198-01-2
1930198019

*This book is dedicated to my beloved mother, Hajar;
and my sisters, Aki and Ashi*

Acknowledgements

Over the past years, there have been many people who helped to make this book a reality. I am indebted to Sue, who was crucial to the birth of this book. She walked with me through my memory with her soul and heart, and we cried and laughed together. I am grateful for my husband, Khosro's unconditional love and encouragement. And special thanks to my oldest son Troy(Hooman) Ghashghaei for his on-going thoughtful advice.

Thanks to: Ali (Arshia) and Ashley Ghashghaei for their generous love and support and encouragement. Sal (Salman) Ghashghaei for sharing and reminding me of his crucial memories in Iran. Ali and Giselle for their support, recommendations and prayers. Mehry and Abbass who helped me as a real sister and brother in the United States. Sue, Alan and Aaron Snyder who filled that void of my family in Iran, and filled many losses from Iran for Salman; Cindy and Dennis Taylor, who were great and welcoming friends in Connecticut, and helped me with my English and to adapt to American culture; And finally to my dear student Zahra in Iran who typed the original text in Farsi.

Thanks to all those who reviewed the manuscript at points in the development: Shahpour Bahrami, Laya and Mitra Gatmiri for carefully reading and sending me great comments, Susan Racher, Maggie Snyder, Aniela Savona, Ali and Ashley Ghashghaei and Sally Rogers.

Sue and I thank our husbands, Khosro and Alan, for their friendship and emotional support, and our sons, Hooman, Ali, Salman and Aaron for reminding us of past events and for inspiring us to write this story.

A huge thanks to Donald Mann for his help in organizing the story, his ongoing encouragement and his appreciation of different cultures.

Special thanks to Diane Somers for her creative suggestions and ideas with the editing of my manuscript.

Thanks to Julie Curtis for her lovely photo portraits and her ability to put us at ease.

Poem by Sa'adi, Great Persian Poet:

بنی آدم اعضای یک پیکرند

که در آفرینش زیک گوهرند

چو عضوی به درد آورد روزگار

دگر عضوها را نماند قرار

تو کز محنت دیگران بی غمی

نشاید که نامت نهند آدمی

Translation of the Poem:

Human beings are members of a whole,
In creation of one essence and soul.
If one member is afflicted with pain,
Other members uneasy will remain.

If you have no sympathy for human pain,
The name of human you cannot retain.

FLOWERS IN MY GARDEN

My Mother, Hajar
> Her mother: Setareh, the shiniest star in the sky
> Her father: Haj Ali (willow tree)
> Her dead son: Parviz
> Her daughters: Aki, Ashi, Mahi (me)
> Her stepmother: Bibi
> Her half-brothers: Latif, Hosain, Hassan
> Her half-sister: Parvin

My Father, Rasoul
> His wife: Farima
> His sister: Esmat
> Esmat's husband: Zaki
> Zaki's brother: Yadi (who became Ashi's husband)

Shazdeh: The master of the Qajar family
> His daughter: Malak-Banoo
> His twin sons: Parviz and Bahram
> His son-in-law: Davood-Khan (Malak-Banoo's husband)
> His grandson: Majid (Malak-Banoo's son)

The Neighbors
> Ali-ba-ba: Shazdeh's gardener
> Mash-Reza: Neighbor's gardener
> Dr. Dashti: A local doctor, available to everyone
> Children of poor neighbors: Zahra and her baby sister,
>   Fatimah, Narges
> Daughters of rich neighbors: Gilda, Beeta and Vida

Political Figures

Dr. Mohammad Mossadeq (1882-1967): *dissident Prime-Minster imprisoned by the Shah in the coup of 1953.*

Mr. Mahdi Bazargan (1907-1995): *dissident Prime-Minister, trusted by Dr. Mossadeq, imprisoned by the Shah and later became a Prime Minister after the Revolution (1979) for nine months, and resigned amidst the U.S. hostage crisis.*

Reza-Khan, later became Reza Shah Pahlavi: King of Iran from 1925-1941.

Mohammad Reza Shah Palavi: King of Iran from 1941-1979, overthrown by the Ayatollah

Ayatollah Khomeini: Revolutionary Leader of Iran from 1979–1989.

Young Adult Acquaintances

Behrooz, Shahla, Mehry, Abbass, Gretel, Katty, Bahman, Fariborz

My Husband

Khosro

Nine Rubies

Ali, Eeraj, Touraj, Ramtin, Ramin, Kamran, Hooman (Troy), Arshia (Ali) and Salman(Sal)

As I sit in the airplane heading to Paris, I put my hand on my tummy feeling the 5 month old seed growing there, and I imagine myself as a mature, happy plant in the garden under the willow tree. My heart shines, and I feel my proud grandfather watching from above.

Then I think, "Where is my home?"

I hear a clear strong voice.

"Your home is within your body.
It grows in the sun and sleeps in the dark.
Wherever you go, the green paths are your passages,
and you might seek your abode through the curving walkways,
and you collect the fragrances of the earth in your garments."

Then I think of joyousness in my home. The willow tree dances gently in the breeze, and the voice comes once again,

"Your joy is your sorrow unmasked.
And the selfsame well from which your laughter rises was

oftentimes filled with your tears.
And how else can it be?
The deeper that sorrow carves into your being, the more joy
   you can contain.
Is not the cup that holds your wine the very cup that was
   burned in the potter's oven?
And is not the lute that soothes your spirit, the very wood
   that was hollowed with knives?"

—from Khalil Gibran

We arrive in the village of Daroos in the north-east of Tehran, and walk about two miles in the narrow streets. Water is running in a small stream beside the pavement, with old willow and maple trees growing naturally by the stream, as they have been for hundreds of years. The smell is of a little water sprinkled on dry soil—a fresh, warm, earthy scent. Residents come here in summer, where it is deliciously comfortable and cool all year round—birds welcoming everyone with their songs. Wealthy and influential people have chosen this area for their summer residences, although some live here all year.

In the valleys we pass small, poor houses close together, and then a farm with a mansion and many acres of land. The townspeople work in the homes and gardens of the rich, and in the local farms. When their work is done, they socialize in the street by their doorways and welcome our arrival with smiles and happy faces that make us feel immediately at home.

We reach a huge wooden door. We knock and a servant opens the door. We enter a beautiful garden with long paths arranged in a delicate design, many trees, and the ground covered with tiny, clean pebbles. As we walk, the whisper of our steps is relaxing and our tension melts away.

Plants are everywhere. Strawberries cover a patch, many cherry trees flourish, and as we get closer to the central pool, there is a huge weeping willow tree. It seems to guard the entire garden, wrapping its branches spiritually around me with unspoken power and love. Under this tree is a round table and four chairs on one side, and a wooden chaise covered with a beautiful red carpet on the other. The pool is a pond that doesn't invite people to swim, but is the home to huge, pregnant goldfish surrounded by many baby fish. Tadpoles and frogs live there, and green water plants reach down into the depths of the pond, visible through the water's clear surface. It is a beautiful blend of nature and human design, wild nature tamed to serve a civilized family.

We see poppies in one round area, ready for cutting and harvesting the seeds. Hundreds of red and white geraniums grace the walks and pathways. Fragrant jasmine climbs the walls, creating a tapestry of welcome. Outside the garden's long walls surrounding the yard are huge evergreens that provide gentle, strong protection.

I hear the cardinals conversing with one another, providing a gentle dialogue. The breeze invites me to dissolve into nature. The spring by the pool whispers calm thoughts in an unending massage to the senses. Tiny blue violets look beautiful and smell like heaven. They are in love with the spring, and lie in its arms to watch the water flow by.

As I move away from the pool toward the house, the steps are covered with large vases with jasmine and white and pink paper flowers (bougainvillea). Between them are fragrant purple flowers with leaves for making tea. The steps are made of natural stones, and there is a beautiful, massive door to enter, with a colorful glass mosaic design.

I feel very safe in this place, and everything I want and need is here.

I fall in love immediately with the willow tree, which reminds me of my grandfather, and gives me security and protection. The flowers remind me of my relatives, replacing the biological relatives that other children talk about. The frogs and tadpoles are the school where I am the director—the frogs are parents and the tadpoles are my students. Aki, my oldest and wisest sister becomes the headmistress, and Ashi, my middle sister, is the impatient disciplinarian.

I t was 1952 and I was 6 years old. Mom called us in from the garden to our small room at the end of the house. She asked us to take the trunk through the hallway into the main living room for a party. We carried the trunk out the doorway, through the garden and up a step into the main house.

Mom opened the trunk. She set aside some old legal papers and a 5x7 picture of the man named Rasoul, who I had learned in the recent past was my father. I gazed at the picture at length, noticing the difference between the handsome, proud officer and the broken man I saw when I was 4 years old in 1950, in Hasan-Abad.

She also put aside a small velvet case that held a tiny, delicate handkerchief. I asked to see it and looked at the embroidered, golden writing.

Mom said, "This says 'My dearest, dear Setareh.' It is a remembrance of love."

From the trunk, she took out three gowns, a blue, a green and a red. Also she brought out a shiny, ornate hand-made jewelry box lined with satin. Inside were three small velvet bags, the same colors as the gowns. She began to arrange the clothes on the floor and match the jewelry—sapphire with the blue one, rubies with the red and emeralds with the green one. All of a sudden she closed the trunk and told Aki to lock the door for safety. Then she started her story.

"When my father, your grandfather, Haj-Ali Tavakoli was young, long before you were born, he met Setareh and fell in love with her in their home town Ardebil, in Azerbaijan, a city in Northern Iran. Setare's family had two main criteria for their future son-in-law – education and wealth. She was a delicate, beautiful, well-mannered girl, the only daughter of the famous Satary family. Her parents home-schooled Setareh, and took her to Russia to see the vastness of the world before she married. Setareh and Haj-Ali met in Baku, Russia once again, and their love flamed."

"Haj-Ali studied and worked very hard to become a successful businessman in Baku, Russia. His success was all part of his plan to become worthy of marrying Setareh. So he returned to Ardebil to claim her as his wife."

"At the outset of the Russian Revolution of 1917, he hastily changed his cash to gold and managed to return to his hometown of Ardebil. He had returned a wealthy man so he came after her, and meeting the family demands, they married. With his money and his wife's pedigree, he quickly became a very influential, successful religious and intellectual businessman in Ardebil and the surrounding region."

"In this town on the border with Russia, Haj-Ali built a mansion. Influential businessmen who came to our city stayed in the main mansion because there was no local hotel at the time. There was a large farmhouse, a guest house, a bath, servant quarters, a bakery and other outer houses—a huge compound in a small town. My father hired servants, gardeners, and cooks. All who worked for him were given a share in his company, and he respected them as partners. They had a wonderful and rich life."

"He was heartbroken when Setareh died in childbirth giving birth to me, after only two years of marriage. The wound in his heart never healed, and he spoke often of her."

"Although Setareh died, my father continued to honor and care for her mother, Yasi (Jasmine). He built a place in the garden for Yasi and me to live and she took care of me. I had one of the most kind, warm and love-filled childhoods that anyone could have. Because my father showered me with love and made a very beautiful private life for me and my beloved grandmother, Yasi, he supported me in a way that compensated for my mother's absence. He hired a nanny to breast feed me. He brought teachers home to educate me. Every night he sat by me and prayed and chanted the Qur'an. He walked me through the path of faith and eventually I fell in love with Islam. He was a father who tried to fill the role of a mother at the same time, while treating heart-broken Yasi like a princess. He came at night and taught us both history and philosophy and advised us to respect everybody for who they are, not what they have."

"After two years he remarried a woman named Bibi, only 17 years old and the daughter of a well known family in Ardebil. She was materialistic and greedy more than being in love with Haj-Ali, and married him for the money."

Remembering Bibi stopped Mom's story. A look came over her face, and she said that was enough storytelling and we should now start our party in the living room. We washed our faces and, even though the dresses didn't exactly fit, we put them on with the beautiful jewelry.

Turkish music played on the radio every day at twenty minutes before noon, and it was her favorite music. She gathered us around the big radio in the living room. Ashi's pink, beautiful skin was bathed in that sapphire and dark blue velvet, so she looked like she was swimming in deep, tropical waters. Although we were very careful with these dresses, Ashi was not very comfortable in hers. She seemed agitated and restless, as though she didn't feel that she belonged. She tried to join us, but was not focused and seemed distracted.

When we arrived in the living room, the table held home-made sour cherry sherbet and cookies that Mom usually made only for special guests. The cherry sherbet was the color of pomegranate juice, deep and deliciously fuchsia. Mom had on her Turkish costume, with a *Daereh* (a Persian frame drum with jingles) in her hand. It was the first time I had seen her wear this beautiful skirt with many layers of different pastel colors, full of gathers, like five different long skirts all at once. When she turned around, it was just like the color of flowers. She had a long, jade-green, silk tunic slit down the sides and a white shawl printed with the skirt's colors. She had a small silk scarf, the same color as the tunic, tied around her forehead like a headband.

She timed her entrance as the Turkish music started on the radio. She was playing the *Daereh* and she showed us exotic Azerbaijani dancing. We were shocked that our shy Mother, who rarely had time to talk to us, danced so beautifully. Mom played the drum very well. After a time, we all started to dance with her. I don't know if anyone saw us from outside but they would have thought we were crazy.

We danced for only a short time when "*Azan*," (the call for prayer), played on the radio and stopped us. *Azan* says : "God is the greatest" and asks Muslims to "put everything down and pray to *Khoda* (God) right now." Every Muslim is required to practice *Namaz* (praying) five times a day, exactly at *Fajr* (sunrise), *Zouhr* (noon), *Asr* (mid- afternoon), *Maghreb* (sunset) and *Isha* (before sleep). Mom always obeyed *Azan* immediately and prayed right on time. As a faithful Muslim, she memorized the Qur'an and used it as a reference for her life.

Before conducting prayer, a Muslim has to perform a ritual ablution, *Vouzou* (a physical preparation of washing hands, feet, and face), and *Ja-na-maz* (preparing a clean rug for under the feet and forehead). Facing Mecca, the home of Allah, there is a pledge that this prayer is fulfilling the person's life, reminding her of the duties as a Muslim and preventing her from wrong-doing. *Namaz* makes a person closer to God.

While preparing to pray Mom said, "Aki, you take care of the jewelry and Ashi put all the clothes back into the trunk. These are a precious memory of my father."

Aki packed the jewelry away, each piece in its own bag and all the bags into the beautiful antique box. She took it to the trunk, and we helped carefully put away the dresses.

I see again a bone-white handkerchief, a gift of love from my grandfather to my grandmother, Setareh, which means star. The handkerchief is made of purest, sheer silk with hand painted flowers, outlined in gold and print saying "My dearest dear, you're my everything." He called Setareh "the shiniest star." He saved the handkerchief, a symbol of this

love, to give to his only daughter when she was old enough to under-
stand. This daughter, my mother, saved the handkerchief to share with
her three daughters.

Mom shook her head, sighed and prayed quietly. Although Mom respected the time for prayer until the day she died, she never ever forced us to pray. There was something about the way she prayed that intrigued us. She thoroughly meditated and dissolved into her world of prayer. It seemed like God was right there with her. We loved to pray with her. We stayed with her and said nothing, just repeated what she said,

"In the name of Allah, the most gracious, merciful, praise to Allah.
Praise to Allah for being cherisher and sustainer of the world. Most
gracious, most merciful, master of the day of judgment. Show us the
straight way, oh God, show us the straight way."

I stayed with her and just echoed everything she said. Aki was not that interested; she was in her own world.

The Qajars, the wealthy owners of our home where Mom worked as a housekeeper and servant, had no idea that when they vacationed they gave such a gift of time for Mom to be with her daughters.

There was only one moment that tarnished the day.

Ashi asked Mom, "Where did you get these treasures? You don't have money to keep me with you, so what happened to Grandpa's treasure?"

She didn't yet know what had been stolen from Mom, nor did she realize that the value of these things was in their connec-

tion to our ancestors and not monetary value that would allow us
to live independently.

Although this playful surprise from Mom lasted a very short
time, it was as powerful as anything in my whole life. It was the
most unusual and wonderful party I ever witnessed and I wish it
could have lasted forever.

The Qajar family was still on vacation and Mom was managing the
house, but made time for another family history lesson. She opened
the pages of her memory and continued her story so we would
know of our rich heritage and be able to tell it to our children.

Eventually, Mom's father remarried into a famous, rich family
from his region which had been bankrupted during the political
crisis. His new wife, Bibi, was older than most brides and together
they had three sons and one daughter. Although they lived in the
same family compound, they had completely separate lives. Bibi
felt as though she was competing with mom for Haj-Ali's attention and affection.

Haj-Ali was very strong-willed about Mom's marriage. It
was the custom at that time for marriages to be arranged. His
young assistant, named Vaziri, was Bibi's cousin. When Vaziri
finished high school, Mom was about 12 years old and Vaziri, at
18 years old, asked to marry her. Haj-Ali said that she was very
young, so he promised that if Vaziri continued his education they
would marry when she was older. On Haj-Ali's recommendation,
Vaziri went to Russia to continue his education since there was
no higher education available then in Azerbaijan. Even though
girls married at age 13 or 14, her father kept his promise and
never accepted offers of marriage from anyone else. He was saving

Mom for Vaziri.

About 7 years later, when Mom was 19, Dr. Vaziri came back from Russia still wanting to marry her. Haj-Ali accepted and as was the tradition began to review Vaziri's record. It was easy for a well-known man like Haj-Ali with all his connections to discover that Dr. Vaziri was involved with the Communist Party. He was an active political member on the 20-man central committee that formed in Baku.

Haj-Ali was a strong anti-Communist, Nationalist and religious man. This news was like a knife in his back. He dejectedly retracted the promise of marriage. Haj-Ali, after the death of his beloved wife Setareh, was broken-hearten once again since he felt betrayed by Vaziri.

I could see the pain on Mom's face as she related, "Marrying Dr. Vaziri was my dream, now ruined. I waited for him all my teenage years. I only thought of him, and now it was over. My dream life was vanished."

Nineteen years of age was unfortunately considered old for a woman to marry, so Mom accepted an arranged marriage by her father's decree. Of the three eligible bachelors that offered marriage, she and Haj-Ali chose the candidate Rasoul. He was a 25-year-old man, attractive and talented, newly graduated from officer's training and working in the military.

Rasoul was smart enough to build a career from tough beginnings. He was raised in a poor family that worked for Haj-Ali. He was also an artist with beautiful handwriting and made lovely paintings. He entered the military out of ambition to achieve more than his family lot. He sought to achieve status. Haj-Ali asked Rasoul nothing but to be a loyal and faithful husband to his daughter. Rasoul put his hand on the Qur'an and promised to do so.

Her father gave them a house close to his mansion and sent her old nanny with Mom to the furnished home, which would be the dream of any newly-married girl. As she had learned well from her grandmother she became an excellent housewife. She liked her new life. The first year the newlyweds enjoyed their life together. One month after they married she was pregnant. This made them very happy, but Haj-Ali was thrilled more than anyone when he heard the news. He sent gifts and layette items every month—blankets, summer and winter clothing, furniture, towels, shoes, curtains. He was so happy that the whole of Ardebil knew Haj-Ali was waiting for a grandchild.

In the last month of pregnancy, a scared Haj-Ali, in order to avoid another tragedy, hired a professional midwife from Tabriz, a larger town, to assure that he would not suffer another loss from childbirth. In the middle of a beautiful summer day, in her father's *Andarouni* (private domain) at the mansion, Mom gave birth to a healthy, chubby child with rosy cheeks and white skin.

Mom said, "As you know, we named him Parviz. My father celebrated for seven days and nights, and he fed many poor Ardebil families during those days. Everyone congratulated Haj-Ali first, and then Rasoul."

Haj-Ali and Rasoul both dearly loved this child. Mom's heart was full of gratitude for this gift from God; she could be a mother in place of the mother she never had and give a grandson to her father to carry on his lineage.

Haj-Ali gave her a diamond ring and said, "You make our family and feelings bright and shiny like this diamond."

Rasoul, from the beginning, wasn't good with money. He held his army job and continued to express his artistic talents, holding up his art and writing as a counterbalance to Mom's father's wealth. He had conflicts with Haj-Ali, who wanted to help financially to provide an affluent life for his daughter. Rasoul was not able to provide the life Haj-Ali wanted for his daughter, and he felt humiliated by the offers of help from his father-in-law. The part of him which did not believe in materialism felt that the wealth should go to the community rather than any individual. Even though he was in the Shah's army, he was a socialist, secular man. Later, and in secret, Rasoul became a member of the Tudeh party, which Haj-Ali, as before with Vaziri, hated and criticized openly. The marriage became difficult. Rasoul showed the other side of himself, having problems regulating his emotions.

The Iranian Tudeh party was the Communist party (Party of the Masses *Hezb-e Tudeh Iran*). It formed in 1941 and promoted socialism, while also being manipulated by the USSR for gains over oil rights. Tudeh sought out intellectuals and modern people, especially in the army. The West covertly sabotaged the Tudeh movement, leading to a crackdown in February, 1945. The Tudeh was formally banned, went underground, and many Tudeh followers were captured, tortured, maimed, or killed. Some surrendered, others escaped to Russia and some betrayed their comrades.

Ardebil was at the border of the U.S.S.R. which was run by a communist government. At that time, communism was a dream for young, poor people as salvation for the world's deprived social classes. Being close to the U.S.S.R., hearing about the appealing promise of a better life and about people governing themselves attracted Rasoul, like many other young people. So after estab-lishment of the Tudeh party, Rasoul and many around the border villages joined.

Rasoul's political choice ruined his and our future lives.

From the beginning, Rasoul and Mom were both trapped in a relationship that was bound for disaster. Slowly, the relationship deteriorated. Rasoul emotionally beat her down through disrespect, infidelity and criticism of her faith. Whatever she wanted he did the opposite, as an act of defiance. She was religious and the more difficult things became, the more she prayed.

She said, "Each time I started to pray he made fun of me, and each time I asked why he did it, he said, 'Why don't you ask your God? I'm doing this to you because I have no belief in God. But if you do, have him punish me.'"

She went on, "Trying not to break Haj Ali's heart, even though Rasoul made love to the nanny in front of me to break me down, I pretended our relationship was happy."

We sat in stunned silence as Mom told us things she probably shouldn't have.

At this point we were interrupted again. The gardener called and stopped Mom's story. It was now time for her to go back to work, but I had learned more about my grandfather, the willow tree.

I go to the willow tree, touching each leaf—like Grandpa, like Setareh—to think about all I had learned. I choose one of the sweet white jasmine flowers and name it Parviz—my relative in the garden.

I speak to Grandpa willow, "I saw your beautiful handkerchief with Setareh's name. I feel how much you loved her and how grieved you were to lose her. I promise I'll take care of that handkerchief forever, if Mom lets me. I love your taste and the colors of the dresses and jewelry."

I compare Haj-Ali with Vaziri and Rasoul, "Are you a human or an angel? Mom talked about two devils and an angel—I wonder how much Vaziri and Rasoul broke your heart. How could you care so much about your family and now Rasoul doesn't like us at all? I wish you were here right now in this garden with me."

I look up and, even though it is daylight, that very bright star is peeking through the branches of the willow, barely visible.

I said, "Setareh, I miss you."

I imagine Haj-Ali blowing a scarf across my face with a gentle breeze.

On another day during our summer vacation, Mom told us another piece of her life's puzzle.

"In the fall of 1939, when Rasoul was in the army, before Tudeh was established, he was chosen to be in the Shah of Iran's wedding ceremony. The Shah married his first wife, Princess Fawzieh Farouk, the sister of Malik Farouk, the King of Egypt. After a formal wedding in Cairo, the Shah and his bride returned to Iran for a great celebration across the entire country. Rasoul was very concerned that he and I should appear modern and proper. He bought very elegant fabric for a tailor to design a Western-style ensemble fit for an officer's wife. I was to wear stockings and black high-heeled shoes. The skirt was mid-calf length. He bought a fox stole with the paws, head and tail still on, with a matching hat. All of this was to be ordered and hand made, ready for the ceremony. Then I was to travel to Tehran, stay in an Officer's Club and practice how to curtsey in front of Fouzieh, the new queen. All the arrangements for officers and their wives were managed through the army."

This was culture shock for my mother. Wearing this type of clothing was unimaginable, as she was a very serious Muslim and always kept her body completely covered, with a long scarf covering her head. She realized that her husband expected her to play a role that she could not manage. She was scared, confused and felt trapped.

She said, "When I wore my own clothes—the velvet dresses, necklaces and colorful scarves—gifts from my father; I felt elegant and comfortable. But I wasn't prepared, nor did I desire, to be forced into modern culture."

When the Shah was young, there were not many women in Iran who worked professionally and they were all in the cities. Women in small towns were very traditional. Two years earlier, in 1937, the Shah's father, Reza Shah, had outlawed wearing the hijab and veil in order to create a more modern Iran. This caused a huge uproar as women and their husbands defied the order. Some women stayed inside for months, and others went out in full cover, risking beatings and having the veil forcefully torn from their heads.

Mom went to ask for her father, Haj-Ali's, intervention.

To her surprise, he showed a very positive attitude and said, "This is an adventure that you should embrace. Go ahead and don't be afraid. I am very excited for you to experience something new. You can't stay stuck in the past and must travel with the times. Life is changing, and if you stop, you're not going to improve. You're not going to know the new world. And you will ruin your marriage and your life."

Haj-Ali quoted from the Qur'an, "To gain knowledge, travel around the Earth."

He always taught Mom to respect every new and different idea and that her strong roots could let her be tolerant of other ways. Mom insisted she not go but her father encouraged her. He paid for a servant to accompany them to Tehran and take care of her one year old son, thinking that he would save his daughter's marriage which he knew was in jeopardy.

So Mom decided to go but she made all arrangements in secret, because in their small town if people knew that she was going to take off her hijab and go to the Shah's wedding they wouldn't approve.

Finally everything was ready and they left for Tehran to be in the celebration. On November 2, 1939, the Shah (then crown prince of Iran) and Princess Fawzia returned to Iran after their royal wedding in Egypt. Now was the time for a huge, Iranian-style celebration. The newlywed couple settled in a palace and rehearsed the Iranian wedding ceremony. Outside, the streets were decorated with lights and green, leafy arches, stretching from the palace to the largest stadium in Tehran (Amjadiyeh) with a capacity of 25,000, where the celebration took place. Everywhere banners flew, welcoming the royal couple back to Iran. The wedding began in the stadium with the playing of the two countries' national anthems. The crowd screamed, "Long live *Valiahd* (Long live the Prince)."

The party continued with classical orchestral music, then a sports exhibition, followed by folk music and local dances performed by students from all over the country. At night the highest ranking guests went to a party at the palace and officers with their wives celebrated in the officer's club. Such a wonderful event, but not for Mom.

She had spent several days preparing and practicing for the upcoming ceremony. For such an important event everyone practiced the protocol, so there would be no mistakes. Two or three days of practice would not force modernity, but everyone tried to enjoy the new challenge. The modern clothing and high heels for the celebration were unusual for most of the women attending the wedding ceremony, and Mom didn't sleep well because she was afraid she would fall and everyone would laugh at her. She also felt the hijab was warm support and without it she felt naked, unfeminine and disrespected. My father was trying to be a modern man and my mother was tied to tradition.

Because my father, Rasoul, came from a poor upbringing the opulence of the wedding was offensive to him. While it could have provided an opportunity for his advancement, it instead made him more vulnerable to the emerging populist sentiment bubbling up in the country. And having the nanny, Farima, traveling with them was distracting because she was beautiful and he was a philanderer. While the nanny gave Rasoul respect and extra attention, Mom had a new baby to care for and was financially and emotionally independent. Rasoul could never find a way to dominate her spirit. Eventually they would separate, and Rasoul would find his way back to the nanny, Farima. That royal wedding did not last "happily ever after," for the Prince and queen, or for Rasoul and mom.

I wander to the willow tree, the grandfather I know so well. No matter what, the willow is the Prince of the garden.

Walking along the paths, I think about how Mom always compared her life with Princess Fouzieh, the previous queen of Iran. By the time the Shah had his first daughter, Princess Shahnaz, my mother had Aki. She frequently compared her husband and children with the Royal family. The white and purple gladiolas wave regally as I pass.

The tendrils of the wild trumpet vines reached toward the tall evergreens, seeking to grow outside the protective boundaries of the garden.

I think about Mom's adventurous side that loved the experience in Tehran. It changed the lives of her future children because she embraced modernity. I think about how the Shah's wedding changed my father, Rasoul, his relationships, and how conflicted he must have been. Like natural grass growing between the cultivated rows of flowers, he sought the natural order of things, without realizing how it damaged the planned organization.

ne year after Parviz was born, Mom gave birth to Aki, my oldest sister, in 1941. Haj-Ali gave her the beautiful green velvet and embroidered gown along with emerald earrings and a necklace. And he said, "You honored our family with this queen. Green is the color of Faith. God bless this child."

Mom said, "One day, three days after Aki's birth, while I was still recovering and not feeling myself, your father took me to a local notary public and had me sign some papers. I didn't know what I was signing, but I trusted him. In that one moment, your father had me sign away much of my heritage, my land and wealth, through this legal maneuver. Here are the papers I signed."

And she spread them out for us to see.

While Rasoul was outwardly in the Shah's army, underground he was involved with the resistance; he had become more and more involved with the Tudeh party. And he spent this money, Mom's heritage, for his loyalty to the Tudeh—he just gave it all away.

Two years after Aki, Ashi was born in 1943. Again the same gift of a gown and jewels, but these were the color of blue sapphires, the sign of the Sky and Life.

And three years after that, Mom gave birth to me, in 1946.

Mom said, "Mahi, do you know that when your Grandpa saw you, he said, 'Oh, this child radiates energy like the sun,' and he gave you rubies, and a red dress. Red is fire, like the sun."

The year of my birth, Iran became politically unstable.

The ideological difference between the Iranian religious nationalists and the socialists was played out in our family. Haj-Ali was a religious nationalist and Rasoul was a Communist and supported the Tudeh; each opposed the other strongly. While Haj-Ali saw the sun when he first saw me, my Father thought I looked like the full moon- especially because I was not a boy. Grandfather gave jewels as spiritual symbols and as a promise, supporting Mom. However, Father resented the show of prosperity, as his party rejected wealth. The two men avoided each other; Mom and her four children were caught in the middle. Slowly Rasoul gave his complete loyalty to the Tudeh, emotionally abandoning his family.

Before Haj-Ali died, he often had his grandchildren into his house to visit and enjoy. Parviz was the only boy heir and he doted on him. So when Parviz died at five years old from a childhood disease, it stole much of the life left in grandfather. And Parviz's death was another huge tragedy in Mom's life. She blamed herself for this disaster, thinking that if she had paid more attention to Parviz' illness perhaps he would still be alive. The chaos of childbirth, raising very young children and a husband who was politically involved in the underground, along with the conflict between her husband and father, made life overwhelming. My father, her husband, Rasoul, was still intimately involved with the nanny and flaunted it in front of Mom. Mom was tormented and torn in many directions.

Haj-Ali was ill and passed away in 1946, heartbroken still from the loss of his first wife, grandson and country. On his deathbed, Haj-Ali said to Mom, "Sometimes God gives you something and then takes it back. So you have to accept whatever happens, and you cannot fight with destiny. But if you show God you're a good person and are grateful, you'll fulfill his promise. The way I raised you, I know you will always take care of your three daughters. I curse your husband, and he will not take care of you. So I appeal to God to watch over you and your children, and I ask you to sacrifice your life for them. I hope you can raise them with the dignity and the wealth I am going to leave for you. If you stay strong and you don't lose your faith, I'm sure you're going to make me happy wherever I am."

"You're going to have 9 grandsons, each as precious as these jewels."

He gave her nine rubies. He died soon after and my mother wondered if she could ever be blessed with nine grandsons, nine rubies.

I am in the garden, thinking, "Where do flowers go when they die? Are they suffering or do they die peacefully? Do they miss the sun, the rain, and the wind? Where do all the birds go when they die?

Heavy wind moved the willow tree's branches and I heard the words of Khalil Gibran:

"For life and death are one, even as the river and the sea
    are one.
In the depth of your hopes and desires lies your silent knowledge
    of the beyond;
And like seeds dreaming beneath the snow your heart dreams
    of spring.
Trust the dreams, for in them is hidden the gate to eternity.
Your fear of death is but the trembling of the shepherd when
    he stands before the king whose hand is to be laid upon him
    in honour.
Is the shepherd not joyful beneath his trembling, that he shall
    wear the mark of the king?
Yet is he not more mindful of his trembling?

For what is it to die but to stand naked in the wind and to melt
into the sun?

And what is it to cease breathing, but to free the breath from
its restless tides, that it may rise and expand and seek God
unencumbered?

Only when you drink from the river of silence shall you
indeed sing.

And when you have reached the mountain top, then you shall
begin to climb.

And when the earth shall claim your limbs, then shall you
truly dance."

I ran was in crisis. Russia was interfering in Azerbaijan to the north and there were tribal uprisings against the communists in the South.

In the town of Ardebil, the political situation became chaotic and extremely dangerous. Less than a month after my birth, on a very cold morning in the winter of 1946, a jeep came to Rasoul's parents' house in Ardebil, the home of my grandparents and Uncle Reza. Mom heard chatters and footsteps of four army soldiers marching toward her father-in-law's house in the alley next door. She started to shake and hide herself to watch secretly from the window. Four armed soldiers broke the wooden door and forced entrance to the house.

They attacked Rasoul's eighteen year old brother, Reza, and beat him and pulled him out, swearing, "You son of a bitch! You Tudehee! You are a spy from Russia! You served a foreign nation under cover! Tonight there will be justice for you!"

Reza was tiny but strong. He screamed, "Stop! Stop! I'm not even Tudehee!"

They didn't listen. They grabbed him, put a rope around his scrawny neck and pulled him to the old pine tree in front of the house.

Reza's parents were crying and begging them to stop but the four soldiers ignored them, focusing on the 'biggest job in the world.'

The parents said, "He played a lot under this tree. He's just an innocent boy! Let him go and leave us alone!"

They pushed the parents away and hanged Reza from the old tree where he used to play.

They shoved the parents into the house with their drawn weapons and said, "Give this message to Rasoul, your oldest son."

Rasoul had a more important role in the Tudeh and therefore was being hidden when the army came into town, so the soldiers were able to find and execute his younger, more vulnerable brother.

As a warning to the Tudeh's the soldiers wrote with a knife on the old wooden door: "Long live The Shah, Death to Tudehs." Then they left in their army jeep.

The tree cradled Reza in its arms and cried with his parents and the whole city that night.

Mom got the message and was terrified because she knew Rasoul would be next. He was hiding in the basement where they kept the coal. That evening, once again, armed men forced into our house looking for him. They looked everywhere but couldn't find him. They entered and searched the yard, then opened every door searching each room. They went to the outside kitchen in the yard and finally went to the storage room where the coal was kept for the winter.

My mother had covered Rasoul with a black chador and hid him in the coal. It was dark, and although they were looking right at him, he was totally covered by the chador, and they didn't see him.

Mom carried me around following the soldiers, with Parviz, Aki and Ashi following her.

She finally hollered at them, "Do you want more blood? I'm so tired. Let's go! He is not here! Look at this tiny baby! Please leave us alone, for God's sake. Look at my terrified children!" She pointed at Parviz, Aki and Ashi.

The soldiers all spoke Azari Turkish.

"Sister," they answered, "You don't know how devilish these Tudeh are."

And they left.

After nightfall, Rasoul came out, covered himself in a black chador and black veil like a woman, and rubbed his face and hands with charcoal so at night he was almost invisible. Mom gave him some money and jewelry. Then she waited until her children were distracted and stood at the door to watch and help him escape. He ran away without even saying goodbye to his children to protect them in case the soldiers ever came back to ask questions. Later we found out he went to a safe hideout using addresses Mom had previously provided from her father's records, and eventually found his way to Moscow.

Mom knew in her heart that Rasoul was more committed to his party than his marriage and children. She wanted a divorce, but even though she had already signed away half her wealth in order to have him divorce her, he never did so.

He said, "I'm going to leave you alone until your hair gets white like your teeth!"

This would prove to be a burden for most of her life. As a married woman, she was never allowed to be free, even though they were totally separated. He, on the other hand, continued to have all the privileges of a Muslim male and was able to have another wife and new family.

As we later sat under the willow tree with her, drinking tea, Ashi, Aki and I asked Mom, "Why did you help him escape? Why didn't you let the army take him to the prison?"

She said, "That was the first test from God. Although he made life miserable for me, his life was in danger and I couldn't let him be killed."

The sky is very dark, and Rasoul is hiding in the sky. I walk through the garden and wonder, "Why are people so miserable to one another?"

I see branches hanging from the tree like dead bodies and all the stars are crying, trying to find a place to hide themselves so they can't witness the death and destruction that is impossible to comprehend.

Now I wonder, "Can I change my surroundings? Is there a better world where I can escape?"

I hug the willow tree branches and comfort them, like they are my scared babies. They are so afraid. I ask the stars to show themselves to me, and not be afraid of the dark world. We all can escape and be safe. I search for the shiniest star, my dear Setareh.

She winks at me, and gives me hope for change.

Mom was a strong and determined woman. Her stepmother, Bibi, only seven years her elder, took all of Haj-Ali's wealth, including my mother's inheritance, to Tehran, along with her three sons and a daughter, Hasan, Housain, Litif, and Parvin. Mom was left with three daughters, and no resources. She said life was empty after losing her husband, son and father.

"I was numb. I didn't have any feeling. It was like being a robot because my whole life had crumbled," she said.

Ardebil, and most of Azerbaijan, was under attack from Russia. Everyone was escaping. Rasoul's political affiliation made it dangerous for us to stay in Ardebil. In the spring of 1946, at 30 years old, Mom had no choice but to escape Ardebil and go to the capital, Tehran, where her stepfamily and all her resources were.

She gathered whatever she had and left behind her beloved town and her childhood comforts. Three children were too much for her to manage alone, especially because she didn't speak Farsi, the official language of Iran. She planned for Ashi and Aki to each leave with a trusted family friend. Then my mother and I boarded the train together.

Aki came safely with my aunt and other relatives, but Ashi was not so lucky. What happened to Ashi on the trip changed the course of her life. At three years old, she was raped repeatedly on the train, with a hand held over her mouth, until the she arrived in Tehran.

Ashi said, "He was a relative of our father, Modiri, a married businessman with four children who used to work for our grandfather, and travelled often between Ardebil, Tabriz and Tehran. He was short and chubby, about 40 years old. Ashi remembered the old army-type train with individual compartments, the cold cabin, a small window with condensation and the sound of "Choo, choo, chooooo!" Then she remembered his army green overcoat and smell of cologne, his rough skin and blonde moustache with a very scary look that sometimes was also very kind. His breath smelled of alcohol and it nauseated her. She saw that he had a small bottle in the chest pocket of his overcoat that sometimes he forced into Ashi's mouth.

"I hated it—it tasted like medicine and made my tongue burn."

She remembered a wooden bench and penetrating pain and hurt. She was scared to death when she saw her private parts bleeding. She said that sometime between light and dark, when the train stopped for people to relieve themselves, she went to the bathroom and when she tried to pee she screamed from the bottom of her heart. She wanted Mom, she wanted her mommy.

"When I came out some people were looking at me strangely and he was waiting there for me. Then he took me to a small *chaikhonah* (a tiny coffee shop) and bought me tea."

Then she said she was scared and cried for Mom, so went to him and hugged him to be safe. He gave her a *ab-nabut* (Russian candy) for her to be quiet.

She said, "Then I was quiet for 30 years."

In spring of 1946, post-World War II Tehran was not a safe place to live. There was a recession and a person's worth was measured by wealth rather than hard work and integrity. For a woman, being a blue collar worker or servant was less respected than a prostitute. Left alone to raise us, Mom turned to her stepmother and two stepbrothers. Her stepmother, Bibi, conditionally invited her to come and live with the family. The condition was to give up her three children to a foster home.

She refused.

At that moment, she made a choice to disconnect herself and her children from the past, even though she was not legally divorced. She told the officials in Tehran that she had lost all her children's documentation in transit, so she could apply for new birth certificates without our father's last name, to protect us from his last name because of his political involvement. She gave each of us a different last name.

Mom contacted a woman who had worked for grandfather and now lived in Tehran, working in a glass-washing factory. There was no plastic at that time and bottles were reused again and again. Through her and some friends she investigated the possibilities. She thought it was an option that two girls could stay with friends and she would take me, still a baby, to work in the factory with her. But the factory rejected this plan.

A 60 year-old widower colonel who was her friend's landlord

saw the situation and offered to marry her. Even though she was 30, she thought that would be a salvation for the family. Then she realized that she was not divorced nor widowed, so the option was impossible by law. This was only requisite for women, as men could very easily marry a second wife, or carry on with one woman while married to another.

Mom took the job washing glasses and bottles in a factory. She rented a room in a house nearby and we lived there several years. Mom had moved from her father's mansion into a single room in someone else's house. The landlord's wife helped out with me as a toddler—they didn't have children of their own so they welcomed us. During the day, we three girls played with homemade sock dolls with makeup features and enjoyed each others' company.

It was not uncommon for us to witness the old landlord in the house nude and having sex with his young wife. After Aki and Ashi went to school during the day, they took me to bed to witness their pleasure. This made me very uncomfortable and I hid under the sink or went outside and pretended that I lived in the street rather than belonging to this house. I wanted to be invisible. It built a sense of shame for my body and diminished my sense of self-worth. It taught me to pretend, to be two people at the same time, ignoring the things I didn't want to acknowledge.

Mom worked at night and came home each morning with little scratches and cuts all over her hands. When I asked, she said, "Oh, Mahi, this is from my new job."

She didn't have anybody, so we were the only ones for her to tell how bad, how difficult, how awful her life was. I cried so hard every night when I went to bed. My sisters and I felt terrible when she complained about her pain, but we always hid our crying from one another. Crying was my bedmate.

Walking in the night-time dream garden, along a sweet-smelling curved path, I see myself coming toward me. I feel so lonely and afraid but my other self is just a child and plays innocently. We start to play together and I feel my sorrow melting away in the sweet air. I move closer to my child-self and feel joyfully ignorant of the things I don't want to know.

We are safe in the garden. Our friends are the flowers, and our protector is here.

Education at that time was free for anyone who was interested enough to find out. Mom was very concerned about our education and, although it was not mandatory to educate children, she tried to send us to a good school. Many poor people sent their children to work. She watched and listened and put Aki and Ashi in a very good school in an affluent neighborhood far away from the factory.

She took them to school on the bus from Akbar-Abad to Amirieh every morning when she came home from work, then took care of me during the day. Because I was young, I either stayed with the dirty old landlord while Mom did errands or slept. She returned by bus to pick Aki and Ashi up and bring them home. This was a huge investment of time and money for food, transportation and clothing; she made so many sacrifices, all for the opportunity to educate my sisters. She also started to learn Farsi in the factory. In her own way, Mom shaped our future with her strength and intellect. But we also learned things that were out of her control.

My oldest sister, Aki, was 9 years old when one of her classmates from a famous, rich family came to play at our house and learned about our situation. Her family, the Qajar family with the beautiful garden, offered Mom work as a house manager, in a home where the mother had recently died of cancer

This man was Shazdeh, one of the grandchildren of the Qajar's family. He owned a mansion close to the village, in the north of Tehran, which was rebuilt about 1920. He was a widower with three children: teenage twin boys named Parviz and Bahram, and a 17 year old girl named Malak-Banoo. In this new generation of Qajars who had traveled extensively in Europe, he chose not to remarry and sought a decent, capable house manager to take care of his huge mansion and children's responsibilities. He found my mom. Qujars spoke both Azari and Farsi, an ideal situation that solved Mom's language barrier problem. I was 4, Ashi was 7, and Aki was 9 when we moved to one room in a rich man's house—a mansion with a big gate, the sweet garden and the party living room.

The Qajar dynasty was founded by Agha Muhammad Khan Qajar in 1794, and was overthrown by Reza Shah Pahlavi in 1925. From 1794-1925, the Qajar princes married multiple women (one married 600!), and had many offspring. They travelled as they wished, sold the riches of Iran to their friends in other countries, mostly Russia and France; and generally raped the country. Even after WWII had damaged Iran deeply, some still lived like royalty. The descendants of the Qajar family, numbering in the thousands, all had access to the Royal Treasury and lived a grand lifestyle. Their mansions dotted the landscape and required servants to maintain the rich tradition.

The Qajar's large villa had lovely, traditional Persian architecture with high stone walls to keep it out of sight, and a beautiful, fenced, private garden with many plants and some huge willow trees. We lived in a single room at the end of the mansion, opening onto a garden that was about 6 acres of land. I grew up in this place without any feeling of belonging, like I was watching a movie in which the house was the setting and I was an actor. The house wasn't really mine, but I loved being there.

Inside, the house was divided between public and private domains. It was decorated with mosaic and mirror work, high ceilings with crystal chandeliers, ornate painted frames and elegant French furnishings. More impressive was the large garden with wild plants, trees, flowers, with mostly wild landscaping, a natural spring and a man-made pond. Unlike in the house, I felt secure in the garden. When I went into nature, I was free.

The garden was my real home because I preferred it to that little, single room our family occupied. Although there was no objection for me to go to any room in the house, I didn't feel that it belonged to me. I pretended that the garden was my real house. Everything in the garden was a relative—stones, plants, water, birds. I named them and made relationships: my big cousin, my little cousin; and I never felt lonely with them. Every flower, bird, fish and frog had a special first and last name. There were family feuds, tea parties and weddings with the jasmine flowers. My best friend was Jasmine. I was told that if I picked the jasmine, it would flower again. I was careful to only pick the jasmine, washing the blossoms in the pond and putting them on the sand to dry.

Sometimes I brought Mom's prayer rug out, washed the flowers and myself, then sat under the willow and prayed like my mom. Grandfather Willow was always there to protect me, and to watch over all of us. When I had a question, I had someone to go and talk to—my wise, Grandfather Willow.

In the garden, nature did not make me feel shamed or dirty. I was secure.

Every summer Shazdeh's family went to France for vacation. I was very curious where France was. Is there a place more beautiful than here? Why do they love Paris so much? They always brought back black and white pictures to show everybody and talked about Paris a lot, so part of me wished to go with them.

On the other hand, in their absence summer was a great time for my family to be together. Usually at this time Mom brought Ashi, my middle sister, home to join us and we could share all our memories with her. Mom, as the Qajar's housekeeper, also oversaw a cook, a gardener and a male servant. This was a huge job and she worked from early morning to late at night. When the Qajars went to Paris for vacation, it was vacation for the workers also, except for the gardener and Mom, who took care of the house. So we had the mansion for ourselves for the whole month. This was when our private parties would occur.

My two sisters were very different from one another. Although she no longer lived with us, Ashi had no limits. She did whatever she wanted. 'No' meant nothing to her. But she was kind, smart and very funny. Ashi filled me with curiosity and let me be free, and I could be adventurous with her. Aki was wise, loving and mothering. She was my role model and fed my curiosity with her knowledge; she taught Ashi and me to be cautious around other people.

One day Ashi and I were playing and Aki was reading a book. Mom was taking care of the whining cat, who was about to have kittens. Mom put an old blanket and a sheepskin in the bottom of a box, forming a makeshift bed.

Then she called the cat, "Come on, pshhh, I made this warm box for you." She put the box at the far end of the garden, in an outside kitchen that was used for big parties. Ashi and I ran to watch, but Mom said we had to leave or the cat would get nervous.

Ashi asked me, "Mahi, do you know where the babies come from?" I had never thought about this.

I said, "No."

She started to explain, pointing to my private parts and singing a little tune. As we got near the pond, close to Grandfather Willow, she started to pull and break the branches and avoided eye contact with me. She knew she was doing something bad. However, Ashi didn't know that tree was my dear grandpa. I tried to stop her, and we got into a fight. I didn't want her to touch the branches. That was when she ran backwards, away from me, and fell into the pond.

The gardener was raking around the garden. I saw him and called at the top of my voice, "Ba-ba Ali! Help!"

As he ran toward us, Aki and Mom rushed over too. He grabbed Ashi's clothes with the rake and pulled her out of the pond with all his strength. He lifted her up, put her tummy on the top of his head and, with her arms and legs hanging over the sides, started running around the pond. I was crying for him to put her down, but Aki said that he was getting the water out of her stomach. I saw the water pouring out of her mouth and then she started crying. Her eyes were wide open with fear. Before this, I thought the gardener was mean and didn't want me around the trees and flowers. Now I started to like him because he saved Ashi's life.

The next morning, we walked outside of our one-room living space to see the cat. Mom brought milk and bread and fed the cat,

which looked very drained and bloody. Mom was sitting by the cat
and feeding her. There were two tiny kitties, licked clean, and one
small kitty body with no head. That scared Ashi and me.

I said, "Look, one doesn't have a head."

Mom said, "I've seen this before. It happens when the animal
is out of energy and needs to protect itself, this is an instinctual
behavior for animals."

Ashi said, "Oh that one is like me."

Mom was shocked and said, "Bite your tongue, you stupid
child. What a harsh thing to say. You broke my heart."

Mom started to cry hysterically, covered her face with both
hands and ran toward our little room.

Aki rushed to us and asked, "What happened?"

I said, "Ashi said something very stupid and made Mom cry."

Mom locked us out. I ran to make *gol-gov-zaban* (special tea);
Aki went to find the holy Qur'an and rose water; and Ashi kneeled
behind the locked door and begged Mom to forgive her.

"I didn't mean to hurt you like that. I don't even know what
I said. I just said what came to my mind," said Ashi.

That was such a heavy day.

Finally Mom stopped crying and let us in. She sat for a while,
and then accepted our offer of tea and rosewater. When she felt
better she looked at Ashi.

"Oh, my sapphire baby, don't get upset. It wasn't your fault.
It was destiny."

My curiosity rang out: "Why did you call her a sapphire
baby?"

Aki shouted, "No 'why' now! Let Mom feel better. Don't ask
her any questions."

After 3 years living together in our tiny quarters at the end of the huge mansion, Shazdeh made a new condition. Mom could only keep two girls. Someone had to go. I don't know why.

It could have been the political situation that limited funds, or perhaps we were just getting older and attracting more attention from the local boys and men. Aki, at 12, attracted attention with her beautiful body and mature, outgoing personality. Ashi was more beautiful than Aki, and very sexy. She was only 9, but she was also a handful and caused many troubles.

I overheard the discussions between my mother and Shazdeh. They were very open with their conversation about abandoning one child while I pretended to play. I don't think they knew that, even though young, I understood what they were talking about.

Shazdeh said, "I don't want to lose you. Go find their father. Maybe he can take care of one of the girls."

The idea shocked my mind: "God, I don't want to be the one left out." And I cried at the thought of being separated. I thought, "If she takes care of me, I will take care of her for the rest of her life." Now I realize how selfish I was, but I did keep that promise.

So Mom started to search for my father. She asked friends from the past and discovered that he had returned from Moscow, perhaps with amnesty from the military, changed his name and opened a small fresh fruit market in Hasan-Abad Square. Hasan-Abad Square, constructed in the early 1300s, had been restored by the Qajar dynasty and featured four identical buildings like an Italian castle. It was a bustling, modern area with paved stone streets, criss-crossed with walkways and lined with metal speed bumps to slow traffic.

Without a job Mom would lose all of her children. She had to make a terrible choice to leave one with the man who ruined her life. She hated to go to my father but without any other help she had no choice. She didn't trust him, and yet he could be their daughter's only savior. There was no time to lose, or she would lose her fragile job situation. She was in a rush, and I grabbed her chador, running after her.

We stopped in front of his small store, with fruits and vegetables on the street in boxes. At the doorstep, Rasoul came out and leaned against the wall. This was the first time I had seen my father, because when he left Ardebil I was an infant. I was shocked to see my sister Aki's face on a stranger, with blonde curly hair just like hers, but also with blue-green eyes and light skin that made him look foreign. It was like he was not even from Iran. I stared at him, collecting the details of his face—his appearance was so similar to my sister who I loved so deeply and yet he was despised by my mom. How could Mom hate this sweet face?

He did not pay any attention to me, not with a look, a hug or a word after four years. In later years, I realized that this was the moment when I formed the notion that there was no emotional bond between a father and his child. Little by little, I realized what I missed as I saw other children with their loving fathers, and I had a lingering sense of rejection.

My mother asked Rasoul, "Do you remember how I saved your life by hiding you and letting you escape? You left me with four children and took everything. When you came out of hiding I had no sign that you were looking for your children, and you would meet your responsibilities. You stole away my fortune, and I have the letter to prove it."

She was crying and wiping her face with her chador. I was recording all of this in my brain and I can never forget it.

He was leaning against the wall, smoking, and looking as far away as Russia.

"How did you find me?"

"Through my friend, Tahereh."

"So what do you want from me?"

"Why didn't you let us know when you came out of hiding?"

"Who needs me?"

"Didn't you remember you have a wife and three children? Do you know anything about Parviz? Do you remember him? And do you know that our only son, Parviz, is dead? He asked and asked for you as he was dying. But you weren't there to help the poor child! Didn't you care for him at all?"

Mom was crying very hard, so I watched Dad to see his reaction. He was as cold as ice, frozen.

She angrily screamed, "Do you have any God? Do you know God?"

He pointed inside the store, went in and we followed.

"Lower your voice. I never got anything I wanted; what more do you want from me? You always took care of everything yourself, and you were your daddy's princess, so busy with your God. You are a *mariam-moghadas* (holy Mariam). The blessed mother didn't have a husband, so you are the same as her. These children are Haj-Ali's children, not mine. I hated your father. I hated your father's name and his fame and fortune. He influenced everything. Haj-Ali thought he was the God of Ardebil and raised you the same way. I am so happy I am Godless now—I have no God in my life. It's your job to take care of the children, to take care of everybody."

"My father was well respected and always took care of his children, and helped our village."

"With a father like that, who needs me?"

If someone makes fun of your mother you never forget it, and I transitioned from confused and helpless to scared and angry, wanting to help Mom with no idea how.

Rasoul didn't show any emotion at all, and said, "You don't need my support because God and your father's heritage are always with you."

This was a pattern with him, to live in the present with no acknowledgment of his past. His life was such a mess that he couldn't afford to look back into a previous chapter, but simply turned the page. I was confused about how he could be so cold and heartless and still be my father. And I felt helpless to help my mom.

Mom said, "I'm a young woman with three beautiful daughters to care for and no resources. People are trying to take advantage of me. I would never have chosen to see you, but now have to ask you to become the father you need to be. I brought our three children from Ardebil to Tehran and have moved them searching for a corner to be secure. All my resources are gone and I am working day and night to manage with no man in our life."

He said nothing. He may still have been hiding because of his past relationship with the Tudeh party. There were many like him in prison, and he was very cautious to not be visible or connected to the people in his past.

She continued, "I found a secure place to live with three kids, and have provided a good education for them. Now the master of the house has asked me, because it is so crowded, to give one girl away. He wants Aki to get married, give Ashi away and have only one child with me. Aki is not ready to marry; she is like you with a very bright mind. I would give blood to have her continue her education. Poor Ashi is only 9 years old; she is the most worried and difficult child in our family. She needs a stable home, a mother's and father's love."

She now looked at me and hugged me, suddenly aware that I was witnessing this conversation. "And look at Mahi, only 7 years old." She put her head on my shoulder and cried very hard.

"Help me not be separated from my children."

I imagined him saying he was sorry for the past, that he was here now and would take care of us, and Mom wouldn't have to worry any more.

Instead he said, "I, myself, am not in a stable situation. I have a very messy life. I cannot take all of you, but will take one if I have to, if that solves the problem." He said it like he was buying fruit.

Mom was surprised by this, and she embraced this idea; at least he would help her with this impossible situation. She announced the horrible decision that she had already thought through a thousand times.

"I need to keep Aki, because she found the job I now have, and will be expected to stay with me. She was our savior and I need to keep this connection. I must keep Mahi because she is still so young. So I have no choice but to send Ashi to live with you. You have to do for Ashi, what my father did for you."

"Don't mention your fucking father to me any more! Just bring Ashi to me, and go away from my sight!"

He opened the door and pointed the way out.

I thought, "Who is this cruel dog? I hate him."

On the way home, Mom was like a crazy woman, crying and running along the walkway that went from one side of the square to the other. She was shaking; it was hard for her to keep the chador in her hand. With one hand she grabbed me and pulled me along very quickly, and with the other grabbed the chador. Meanwhile she was wiping her nose. I was holding onto her chador not to lose her as she rushed.

She was talking loudly to God, "Do you see what is going on? Where are all the promises my father gave me? Why does all of this happen to me? Where are you? I helped him to escape, gave him money, gave him an address to be safe, and in this special moment when I need him, he rejects me, even though I am still his wife! All men are dogs! I should never have gotten married. I should never have had children. They are so self occupied. Even my father remarried after my mother died. All men are selfish and they want everything for themselves." She wrapped herself deeper and deeper into her chador.

Everyone was looking at us and I was embarrassed. I tied the chador in a knot around my hand and was running after her, scared and confused. Suddenly, I fell down. Sharp, killing pain shot through my arm. My right elbow struck against one of the metal bumps in the road and broke. It was so painful, my mom and I were now both crying like crazy. She took my hand and cared for me, calming me down.

We got on the bus and finally got home. There she put egg yolk on a bandage and placed it on my broken bone, opened the holy book over it and gave me holy water to drink. She put me to sleep.

When I woke up it was a sunny afternoon and Mom was packing. I had been asleep for maybe 18 hours. She said the Qur'an and holy water healed me and made me sleep. When I woke up it was very difficult for me to move my arm. The stuff she had put on the injured area was like a splint, and my arm slowly began healing with the bones out of place. My arm is still out of place at the elbow joint, as Ashi's life is still out of place. We were never totally the same again.

Mom went to Shazdeh and told him that she had disposed of one of her daughters. Then we had a very sad private party and she explained the situation to my sisters.

"Girls, sit down here. I need to tell you what is going to happen."

She then explained her decision.

She said, "Aki is our connection to the Shazdeh's family, Mahi is so young, and Ashi has to go with her daddy."

When she heard the news, Ashi started to cry, "Why me? Why me?"

Aki said, "No, Mom, no, Mommy, there must be another way."

Mom tried to be calm, and said that she loved her. "I will

come and see you every weekend, and you can come here during the summer when the Qajars are in Paris."

Everyone was crying. Ashi became more agitated, started pulling her hair and hitting herself, then went to the corner of the room, covered herself in a blanket, crying softly. Aki took a book and started reading in another corner of the room. Mom started cooking rice, quietly sniffling and trying to hide her sadness. I felt like fainting and went into the garden.

For the next 10 days, it was like there had been a death in the family. It felt like we might die without Ashi or she might die without us. Everyone kept to themselves. Because of my arm, I was mostly in bed and sick. Aki remained occupied with her own books, as she always did, to isolate herself and avoid the real world. Ashi remained secluded and quiet. Mommy started packing Ashi's things and making sure she would have what she needed. We all wanted to give everything we owned to her, so we begged Mom to pack our dresses and shoes for Ashi too. We were not sure we would ever see her again, just as if she were going to the battlefield. Mom was sleepless. Even when she was not working, we could hear her praying and talking to God a lot.

The emotional trauma of forced separation was far more than the physical hurt of a broken bone.

Along the garden walk, I stop to look deeply into a deep ruby-red rose, bursting from a bud, but not yet fully developed. The smell is indescribably delicious, like heaven. She sits beautiful and elegant, petals so soft that silk envies her beauty, protecting herself with sharp, large thorns and thousands of little prickly stickers. The leaves, shiny and strong, embrace the thorns with pride. They dare intruders to touch, knowing there is thorny support just below. The thorns are sharp to the touch, but if you clip one just a little, it becomes as soft as the petals and leaves, showing a gentle inner core. It is there to protect, but not to harm.

The rose is free and independent because it has such strength just beneath the surface.

My middle sister, Ashi, started a new life with my father and stepmother, Farima. Mom worked hard day and night, so we wouldn't look like the children of a housekeeper. She kept us neat, clean, well-dressed, and well-mannered. We were the companions to Malak-Banoo, 21 years old and the family's only daughter. We felt close to her and her father, Shazdeh, the master of the house. This new environment in which we grew up gave Aki and me a feeling of being princesses. We had friends in the surrounding houses, including Gilda and Beeta, two of the Senator's daughters.

One morning in the summer, Gilda and Beeta's father, a government official, didn't go to work. While we were playing, Beeta came out and said, "My father is very upset, so we must play very quietly not to bother him." We went in their house and played quietly. My antennae started to focus on everything I could see or hear.

I saw Beeta's father in his robe, unshaven and looking ill, listening to the radio. He was pacing along the hallways, constantly on the phone. This wasn't normal, and was scary for me. Because I was already an anxious child, and I could feel when things were not right. I was more focused on the father than on Beeta, and when I asked her about him, she became angry. She was frustrated that I was preoccupied, and not playing with her. I couldn't concentrate to play, so I went home to Mom.

I explained the situation to Mom and asked if she knew what was going on.

She said, "Oh God, I hope nothing happens. We don't need war. I don't want to see any executions again. We need peace."

I was so curious.

Mom listened to the radio as she worked, so she knew what was happening. She was a very political housekeeper! She treated me like a political friend, sat me down, and slowly, thoughtfully explained that the Prime Minister, Dr. Mossadeq, was captured, and the Shah had left the country.

She said "Everything is out of control, and people are mobbing and looting Dr. Mossadeq's house, taking anything of value, and saying 'Death to Dr. Mossadeq!'"

During this time I learned about a man who became one of the most influential people in Iran's history. Dr. Mohammed Mossadeq was an educated and truly free-minded man who was raised in the Qajar family. When he was 21 years old, the people of Esfahan elected him to the *Majles* (Iranian parliament). He did not meet the legal age requirement but he actively participated in political events. He graduated in political science from Tehran University, continued his education in Law at the University of Neuchatel in Switzerland and received a Doctorate in Law. Then he returned to Iran. When he opened his office in Tehran, he placed a framed saying of his mother's, who is best known for founding Najmieh Charity Hospital, "*The worth of a person in the*

society depends on how much one endures for the sake of the people."
He kept these words in his mind all of his life, and eventually
became a powerful example through his actions.

Mossadeq had a dream for a free, independent, democratic
Iran. At that time, the British owned 51% of Anglo-Iranian Oil
Company. The British were interfering directly and indirectly in
Iran's political affairs. Mossadeq lawfully fought for Iran's inde-
pendence, including the unfair oil agreement with Anglo-Iranian
Oil Company. All Iranians—religious, secular, nationalist, busi-
ness and the common masses—overwhelmingly supported him,
with the exception of the Shah and his supporters—the Central
Intelligence Agency and British Intelligence. The Shah observed
Mossadeq's rise with trepidation.

On December 1925, when the Shah was only six years old,
his father, Reza-Khan, marched to power and became a crowned
King with the support of the British government. On January 14,
1926, as Reza-Khan's oldest son, he was named Crown Prince, and
was also supported by the British government.

Now, Mossadeq, with pride and heroism, became the
enemy of the Shah and Great Britain, as he led the struggle
for Iran's independence. He led the movement in Parliament
to nationalize Iran's Oil industry. He was supported by most
political and economic groups. The Shah was advised by his
supporters that Mossadeq was aiming to take his power and
replace the monarchy with a republic. Mossadeq maneuvered
the oil nationalization bill through Parliament until finally, on
March 19, 1951, the bill was passed. With the parliament and
public behind Mossadeq, the Shah was forced by the people to
appoint him Prime Minister.

Tension increased between Iran and Great Britain. Winston Churchill, Britain's Prime Minister became Mossadeq's arch-enemy, swearing to remove him before he died. The British imposed economic sanctions on Iran and threatened a military attack. Iranian espionage agents discovered that the British-run Anglo-Iranian Oil Company was bribing Iranian officials to prevent nationalization. In response, the Iranian government closed the British Consulate.

In October, 1951, Mossadeq traveled to New York as Iranian Prime Minister, to appear before the United Nations to defend Iran's right to nationalize its oil industry. He gave a powerful presentation and successfully won the case. This news was covered widely through the world. He also went to Washington DC and met President Truman. By January, 1952, Mossadeq's picture was printed on Time Magazine's cover as the Man of the Year. When he came back to Iran, all the Iranians chanted "Long live Iran, long live Mossadeq."

The Shah watched Mossadeq's takeover of the oil industry and was concerned over Mossadeq's rising popularity. Unloved Mohammad Reza Shah wasn't supported by the people, so left the country in 1953 with a promise from England to return him to power.

The agenda, proposed by the British and planned by joint British and American intelligence, and named "Operation Ajax," was implemented. Mossadeq surrendered and was imprisoned. Of his followers, hundreds were killed or wounded, and many more were arrested, imprisoned, and tortured to death. The reign of terror had begun.

In his trial Mossadeq pronounced: "I am well aware that my

fate must serve as an example in the future throughout the Middle East in breaking the chains of slavery and servitude to colonial interests."

Mossadeq was convicted of treason. He was placed in a solitary cell for three years, followed by home arrest for the reminder of his life, which ended March 5, 1967. Without Mossadeq, democracy died in Iran.

Mom was very afraid, and remembered the Azerbaijan crisis. She was not really talking to me, but seemed to be anxiously speaking to the ally she needed to have at that moment. I was very scared because I was waiting for them to come and execute everybody. Then I asked her if they were going to execute Beeta's father.

She said, "Don't ask any more questions; just don't go out." Insecurity covered me, and I thought perhaps the world was coming to an end.

As the gate was always open to the outdoors, I saw Dr. Dashti, our neighbor, walking. His face was the same as Beeta's father's face—very preoccupied and distraught.

I ran to him and said, "My mom said it is very dangerous to be out and you should go inside."

He took my hand and said, "This valley is safe."

He walked with me a little, looked at me, and said, "God, what's going to happen to these children's future?" Then he was talking like to himself, "I wish we never had this oil in our country because everything happens as a result—dark, black blood in the country's veins."

The way he acted scared me to death. I thought he was going out of his mind. I hid in my room with many unanswered questions and great anxiety from people surrounding me—all of them mourning in their own private quietness, nobody desiring or daring to talk to anybody else.

Dr. Dashti's words came alive in my mind, a monster with black blood in its veins, trying to eat all the children. In reality, it was a coup by the United States against Dr. Mossadeq, against democracy in Iran. Rather than the Mohammed Reza Shah becoming a loved figurehead, he regained the power to form a dictatorship.

I know now that this was the day, the coup of 1953, that democracy was suffocated in my country. It changed Iran's destiny and our personal destiny as well. But at that time, I felt the heaviness in the environment, and only knew it was something bad. People around us were not happy, and all seemed anxious and scared.

I take my questions to the flowers and trees, my friends, and try to calm down. I repeat every event in my life, with each flower taking the role of a character or situation. This is my way to process and understand any threat or fear, because I have no one else to go to.

I imagine whatever I know of the world in the pond's microcosm. The pond's bottom is like the black blood of Iran. The tadpoles are the people, and the biggest frog is Dr. Mossadeq. The goldfish are my family, and the big pregnant fish is Mom. I become lost in time and space as I sit by the pond, and only reenter the real world when someone comes by and calls out to me.

Even today I return to the pond to search for answers. The pond is the way I survive.

When my father returned from Moscow in 1950, he rejoined his elderly mother and three married sisters in Tehran. Later that year he was married to Farima, our former nanny in Ardebil. When Mom came to Tehran, she couldn't manage to take Farima along with her three young children, so she divided us up with family members. Farima was left behind with my father's family, and then traveled with them to Tehran. She lived with them until she finally married our father. This was very confusing, since she had once been our nanny, and Mom's servant. But now she was Mom's equal. Rasoul did not need to divorce Mom in order to marry Farima, because men in Iran didn't need permission for more than one wife. She was nineteen years old, and an illiterate village girl. In Ardebil, my father had used Farima to humiliate my mother by having sex with her in front of Mom. Farima told Ashi that on the way to Tehran she had been raped by my aunt's husband, Zaki, unbeknownst to my aunt, Esmat. Because she was not a virgin, she was forced to remain with the family, with no hope of marriage. Farima told Ashi her dream came true with this marriage.

Now, Ashi was forced by destiny, to live with Farima and my father's family. In the family compound, Aunt Esmat, was the boss. She managed the marriages, liasons, pregnancies, and was the queen of Hasan-Abad valley.

Farima became pregnant every year. Ashi told us later that Farima, with a one-year-old child, was pregnant again. My aunt hollered at Farima not to have any more children, because she already had one. Now Farima was desperate and crying, begging to keep the baby. My aunt and her sisters attacked. One of the sisters sat on her chest and the other sister forced a knitting needle into her vagina. She continued until Farima was bleeding. Ashi was hiding between the pillows in the closet, terrified, trying not to hear Farima screaming. When the aunts finished the job they called Ashi to come and help Farima clean herself, and make her tea to stop shaking. "And if you tell anybody this, even your father, we will kill you!"

Poor Ashi made tea and tried to copy mom to calm Farima down with the holy book and holy water.

Farima liked Ashi but she often became very agitated and angry toward her. Ashi was Farima's scapegoat. Every day she asked Ashi to do more work. If Ashi didn't do enough, she was pulled to the floor by her waist-long hair. Ashi would scream and cry until the neighbors came and took her away. After that, Farima hugged and kissed Ashi and made tea for her. It was a roller coaster ride.

Every night when father came home he was so nice to Ashi, put her on his knee, kissed her and said "You are my little girl. If anyone ever touches you, just let me know. Then I can hang them."

Ashi, of course, denied to others any kind of harm or unfairness because she was told that if she talked to anybody about anything she would be killed.

After a while Farima was pregnant again but didn't say anything until her tummy spoke for her. This time my father knew it and he was happy to have another child.

The man who worked in my garden didn't like me because he thought I was crazy, always talking to the trees and birds. And I was always watching him. I didn't want him to touch any of the plants or take anything away; if he moved a plant it was like taking a child away from its home. Whatever he did in the morning, I changed back before dark.

Every morning he came and yelled, "Who is working here besides me?"

I stayed in the corner and watched him. He probably knew, and wondered why I was so obsessed with the flowers.

When I sat under the willow, it was like I was in my grandfather's lap. It was summer, and I was preoccupied with the jasmine, tulips, daffodils, lots of roses, peonies, johnny jump-ups; they were like new babies, and I pampered them. The only one in my way was the gardener. Although he was taking care of the garden, I didn't want him to change anything. This was a constant conflict between him and me.

Toward the end of the summer he started to cut some of the flowers. I came from school and saw him cutting my cousin's necks—they were roses. I was watching him and started to pray like my Mom, "God, please help me. Why is he doing this? Why is he so mean? Why is he so cruel?"

Then I hid behind one of the big trees and started to throw pebbles at his back, neck and head. They were little and I don't think it hurt him, but he wondered what was going on and where it was coming from. He started to swear and yell, and I ran away to the small room, went to bed and put a pillow on my head. I cried very hard. He cut most of my grandfather's branches and killed all my relatives. He walked on the babies. He didn't care any more that they needed me.

I imagined he was a killer, and the next day I walked out and was devastated. It was like a battlefield; all my relatives killed, some injured and some covered and tied with rope. It was like a big funeral of my friends and family. I walked among them crying but everyone else was too busy to care. Now there were no branches from the willow low enough to hug me in my sorrow.

That was the first time that I got detention in school because I didn't do my homework. The teacher told me I was responsible for the future. Mom tried to make me feel good, but said I must study hard because I was the only hope left. I knew that both of our futures were now in my hands. Mom leaned on me and I knew I had to carry her for the rest of her life, as long as I was alive. While I loved caring for her, I also subconsciously resented it. It was a huge responsibility for a child, and an unnatural role reversal.

The rain came and I thought the sky was also crying. It seemed like God was cleansing my battlefield. I always liked the rain because it made me feel pure, washed away the damages. That garden man sat on the steps having tea. I remember putting two of the little stones in his tea when he was busy, and then I ran away.

It was fall when the gardener explained to Shazdeh that the roots of the willow tree were destroying the pool's cement foundation. Shazdeh said to ask the mason (Hasan-Mason) if he agreed that the roots would destroy the pool. If so, the tree would be cut and the roots burned.

I thought, "Oh, my God, now he wants to destroy my grandfather's roots." I thought only God could fix this problem and save my favorite tree. At night when Mom was praying, I asked her "If I want something from God, what should I do?"

She said, "You have to be a very good Muslim."

I asked her how I could be a good Muslim, so God would help me.

She said, "You must be honest and strong. Don't lie, don't steal, have strong faith in God, and take care of people. Then God comes very close to you and answers you with wisdom. Each time you pray you're talking to God and making yourself pure and ready for God's touch."

I tried to follow Mom's advice. Each time I found myself bargaining with God praying, "God, I'm doing this, but you must do that for me. I don't want you to kill this man, but maybe if he gets sick he won't work any more." Then I thought he might die from getting sick. So I was confused about what I wanted, but I knew I didn't want that gardener anymore and wanted God to save that grandfather tree from Shazdeh.

There was a solarium near the garden, controlled for temperature and humidity, which was a shelter for the remaining plants and flowers during the winter. Jasmine was the bride of the solarium, refreshing my heart. In the village, winter was very cold and the plants were moved into the glass room. We used a wood burning stove and a covered table with coals in it, called "*korsi*." When it was very cold outside, I went under the *korsi* to watch the snow and the solarium. It was the best feeling—very clear—no smog or smoke. I even had a *korsi* in my little room at the end of the garden. When I was so hurt from losing my many flower relatives, I saw this solarium as a sign from God.

When jasmine flowers were blooming, I would pick some early in the morning and put them in my mom's janamas—the small prayer rug with a scarf, rosary and stone for resting one's head during prayer, showing gratitude for the earth. I think this really made her heart happy. No one took care of her things but I did this for her.

One day in the solarium jasmine, my Jasmine, looked very lonely to me. I tried to find some of the flowering plants and put them close to Jasmine. I moved the plants around and felt she was not so lonely.

Then I saw the gardener behind me yelling and swearing, "What do you want from me? Oh, you crazy child. These things need some sun, others need shade."

I told him he had no right to leave jasmine alone there. He took my hand and pulled me to my mom in the kitchen.

He told her, "I don't know what she wants from me. She is always following me and bothering me. And now she has found the flower house and she is changing things. I don't want her to touch the flowers any more or I'll go to Shazdeh. She even put stones in my tea to break my teeth."

I swore to God that I didn't do it to break his teeth, but only to make his tea dirty.

Although his mean words didn't affect me, later I went to see my friends in the flower house but the door was locked. I couldn't get in. So now it was just like a prison. I went to see them through the window. The gardener changed all the flowers I put next to Jasmine. I didn't have any more of those white flowers I loved to smell to put in my mom's janamas.

I remember from that moment I started again to be preoccupied with my family's problems, Aki, Ashi and my Mom. All happiness left me. From that time on I had sad memories. Some children have lots of toys to play with but the garden was my playroom, and my sisters and I invented our toys out of everyday objects. Without the ability to play freely in the garden, my source of imagination disappeared and I had no choice but to stay more in my little room, separated from my inspiration.

I was almost in 7th grade. I started to write down little memories, little letters to the flowers that I could not touch. I went outside, poured gasoline and burned the letters. Burning gave me a relief from my anger.

The next year the gardener said, "If we're cutting the willow tree we should do it in the fall, and then the root will dry during the winter."

I was anxious every day to see what was going to happen, and I kept on praying faithfully.

It was one week before the end of the summer. All the children were getting ready to go back to school but I was obsessed with the willow.

Shazdeh and his family were sitting in the shade of the tree when the gardener came and told Shazdeh, "I have news. Unfortunately, I have to resign. I have to go to the north of Tehran to

Rasht. One of the representatives in Rasht has a job for me to produce rice. Because my wife's parents are very old and live there, I decided to go. It is a big opportunity for me to take care of our parents."

Shazdeh was cold toward his workers, and accepted this news with no emotion.

I was listening to that and realized that God had answered me. The gardener would leave and the tree would be saved. Shazdeh enjoyed using the shade of that tree and he would not remember about the pool. I felt I was a really good Muslim, and thanked God for working this out so well and peacefully. My feeling was that all the plants and trees celebrated that night the way my mom had, dancing with the Turkish music with colors, jewelry and lots of fun. We were all dancing in the garden. Mom had to call me in from my tango with the trees. The following week the gardener left forever and I never saw him again.

When she was pregnant Farima was very lazy and only wanted to sleep. She demanded that Ashi serve her. In a complete role reversal, when the child was born Farima chose Ashi as nanny to her child, as Farima had been to Ashi before in Ardebil. Behind my father's back, Ashi was no longer allowed to go to school. Ashi didn't like school anyway so she didn't mention this to Rasoul, and was secretly happy. The baby became Ashi's doll and replaced school.

Ashi was so happy taking care of the baby. It replaced her school and friends. She felt it was healing her heart from the separation from Mom, Aki and me. One day while Farima was changing the baby's diaper she wanted Ashi to fry onions for lunch. Then Farima gave the baby to Ashi and left for shopping. Ashi was so involved with playing and singing to the baby in the other room that she forgot all about the frying onions on the stove. All of a sudden, when Farima returned she opened the door and black smoke billowed out.

Farima screamed, "Where are you? Where is the baby? What are you doing? You bastard!" Then she turned off the stove, put the baby in bed and with eyes red with anger came toward Ashi.

"Who do you think you are? Huh? I'd just like to know. Who

do you think you are?" And then she pushed Ashi to the floor, rushed to the kitchen and put the hot pan on her tummy. Ashi started to struggle and scream, apologizing.

Farima hollered, "Oh yes, you will be sorry for your whole life!"

Ashi cried hard and was in extreme pain. Farima took Ashi to the little washing pond inside the yard and told her to stay in the water until the pain went away. Then she made tea for Ashi, hugged her and said, "You know, sometimes I'm so mad that my mind doesn't even work."

That night Farima went to Ashi to say goodnight and told her to never mention this incident to anyone. "You know that I like you and I didn't mean to hurt you."

Ashi promised.

She later told me, "I enjoyed that hugging and kissing so much, I wished that she would always remain that way, even though she had beat me and burned me."

At night when my father came home he asked for Ashi, and Farima said she was not feeling well.

"I think she got her first period. Our little girl has to rest tonight—leave her alone."

Some days after, Ashi's belly was almost healed but still bothered her a lot. Helping Farima was painful for Ashi now, especially carrying the baby. One weekend when Rasoul was home, Ashi was stuffing a nylon sock to make a doll while Farima was cooking and busy with her kids.

All the time Rasoul was complaining to Farima, "Make the kids quiet, don't walk like a horse, don't talk too much, you stupid village girl. You never know how to manage the kids."

Ashi wondered why he was so moody today. At lunch,

Farima asked Ashi to put *sofreh* (lunch on a blanket) on the floor and bring the dishes. Although it was very hard for Ashi to bend down, she did her best. When lunch was laid out on the *sofreh*, the younger baby started crying.

Rasoul started yelling, "What's going on in this house? What is all this noise about? What did I do to make my life so miserable? I hate your looks. Why are all the doors closed to me? Look at me, an officer, an artist, with the best drawing and writing, the one who was honored to be in the Shah's wedding, that damned Shah, damned Tudeh! Fuck them all! Fuck the whole world!"

Then he kicked the *sofreh* and food went all over the room.

Farima used to call him *Agha* (Master). "*Agha*, what's wrong today? I didn't do anything bad."

Rasoul said, "That's it. Now you're talking back?"

He rushed to the closet and pulled his leather army belt off his trousers and started prowling around like a crazy man. He hit Farima in the face, hands and feet.

Ashi got between them, begging "Please Father, stop."

Ashi was in a lot of pain and, thank God, our crazy father put her in the closet and said never to come to him when he was angry. When the storm was over, Ashi fell asleep in the closet.

When she woke up she was shivering, crying and calling, "Mommy! Where are you Mom? Please come and take me home. I want to go home."

Usually when Rasoul came home at night, he brought the freshest fruits and his bottle of vodka . He had Ashi sit by him while he was drinking and spoke to her of his memories. One night he seemed very preoccupied with the old days.

"Oh, my motherless child, I'm afraid I'm neglecting you. I am not a good father to all my children. I am not a good person. I am a traitor." He was going on and on and drinking. Then he asked Farima to join him.

He asked her, "Do you really love me?

She said, "Yes, *Agha*."

"Don't be a liar!"

"Of course not, *Agha*."

Then he asked her, "Do you remember my son Parviz?"

"Of course, *Agha*. I was his nanny. I loved him from deep in my heart."

Rasoul continued, "Remember how handsome he was? I taught him the alphabet when he was three. He was very smart."

Then he started to laugh hysterically, "When we wrestled I pretended he bit me. He was extremely proud to win." Then Rasoul burst into tears, "How could I forget his scared look when I was hiding in the basement? When I kissed him good-bye he was crying and begging me not to leave."

Then he sighed, "But I left with no choice. I had to escape the country or be killed." Then he started to cry, lit a cigarette and pointed, telling us to leave the room.

But Ashi remembered her brother from years ago and said, "Parviz was my brave brother. Once a kidnapper came by and he kicked that man and screamed. He made the kidnapper run and hide. I played with Parviz all the time… he was so sweet. He was the only man in the house."

She stroked Rasoul's arm tenderly and continued, "Father, when you left he got sick. He cried and cried for you, he missed you so much and wanted you home. I miss him too, you know."

Living with the Qajar family changed me. I wasn't the same person as the girl who lived in a room by the factory. I became a princess. I pretended that Mom was my fairy Godmother, appearing when I needed her and invisible any other time. Inside I felt conflicted and confused. I loved her but I tried not to be seen with her in public. I could die for her, but also wanted to distance myself from her. I enjoyed the feeling of being a 'pretend' princess, while emotionally suffering from the reality of our lives. The guilt was always with me. Inside I judged myself to be a selfish, bad child.

Everyone around us liked me very much and called me "little princess." Mom was very proud of her little girl, but her best compliment was when she said I was like the son she wished for. A son would save and take care of her for the rest of her life. I became that son for her. She was the source of my perception that being a female was inadequate, but I fulfilled her desire to be supported by a man. My sisters developed the same feelings, an unintended message of inadequacy from Mom. My sister, Aki, told me later that when she went to bed, she always cried under the blanket because she was not the boy that Mom wanted.

Mom could bring Ashi for short visits. Ashi had a free spirit and accepted what had happened to her, but she had a rebellious streak that came from the hard life she was living. She didn't pretend to be anyone else like I did. She was real. I felt that my dear Ashi was totally different than she used to be and I wanted to change her back. Aki and I were taught how to eat, how to walk, how to speak correctly; Ashi was exactly the opposite. I tried to change her but she was older and didn't want to learn from me. She was offended when I tried to teach her manners because she needed to be content with her life as it was outside our family. We had constant conflict between us—love, hate, guilt and distance. I had no control over the situation in which we found ourselves and couldn't accept Ashi.

Our village was small and had just one school. There were rich and poor students mixed—a few rich and more poor. The rich children were treated totally differently than the other children, and I didn't know where I belonged.

I was poor but pretended to be rich because I was coming from the Shazdeh's house to that school, although my mom was a servant. I had the best dresses and a beautiful place to live, so I saw myself as rich and I was accepted by the rich kids. Also knowing my mom's background, I could imagine how it felt. It was very painful because it wasn't real, but I forced myself to imagine that I belonged with the rich children. The rich kids were very fussy and princess-like, and were allowed to have nail polish and different dress than uniforms and were absent whenever they wanted.

If a poor child didn't do their homework they were put in the corner and had to stand on one foot for 10 or 15 minutes. They cried until they were invited back to the group. But the rich kids were excused because of their parents.

The rich kids came over and talked about their parties and guests. I had nothing to talk about—no father and no parties. Secretly I knew my place because I wasn't really like them.

I didn't have the nail polish, nor was I absent, but I was treated by the teachers like the rich children. Still, I took the side of the poor kids when they were treated unequally.

The rich community welcomed me because I was a sweet and well-mannered child; I played my role well. But in my heart I related to the poor children, and thought I could take care of them by influencing the rich. I realized that the poor children's parents were like my mom—in pain. I tried to help by giving whatever I had to them, and when the rich kids were making fun of the poor kids, I didn't join in. I tried to protect and support them, whenever possible, and be respectful of their families.

Lunch was very different for the rich and poor children. Sometimes the rich children had hot meals delivered by servants. Their parents also often provided food for the teachers, which made the teachers grateful to these families and more kind to their children. The poor children brought some bread and perhaps some cheese and dates, or whatever was left over from dinner. When I brought lunch to school, I shared with the poor children. The rich and poor ate in different parts of the hallway or yard, and I went to the poor side. This was when I felt totally connected to the poor children.

So, I was accepted as a leader in both groups: the rich children liked me because I was smart and doing very well in school; the poor children really liked me because deep in my heart I was like them. I enjoyed going to their houses to visit and play with them, and enjoyed their moms too.

One day when I went to school there was a new government program that provided nutrition in school for needy kids. The headmaster came outside and announced that the program was beginning, so kids who thought they needed it could register to get milk and yogurt every day. I would have loved to have milk and yogurt at school, but I didn't register because I followed the rich children's behavior. It was good not to feel needy.

Later on, our neighbor's gardener's daughter, Zahra, came to me and asked why I didn't register. I said, "No, I'm not poor."

She said, "Why don't you register, then give the food to me for my little sister at home?"

I agreed. I registered, telling the teacher, "This is for Fatimah, Zahra's sister."

The teacher asked who she was, and told me I could only register for myself. I told her I wasn't poor, but Fatimah needed this food. The teacher asked if I knew the rule. I said yes, the program is for needy people and we could help Fatimah, who needed it. The teacher said that it was only for the kids at school and that I couldn't take the food out of the building. When I asked who made that rule, she told me I was a fresh child and she didn't have to explain to me who made that rule. I suggested that no one would know if she and I made a new rule right then.

If I registered, my name would always be announced with the welfare kids and this status would follow me into my future. I thought I was doing the right thing, even if it was going to hurt me. The teacher was frustrated with me and asked me to leave her alone.

My headmistress's husband, Dr. Dashti, was average height, trim, bald, with a kind but distinguished face. He had a little moustache and big, thick glasses. When he looked at you he seemed to offer help with just his glance. He wore a brown suit with a stethoscope sticking out of the pocket, a white shirt and a light red tie. He wore old, dull shoes. He had very strong, long hands and fingers, too big for his body. He was very kind to me and always called me "my child." I always felt distance between the headmistress and me, but Dr. Dashti was much nicer.

I couldn't help thinking of Zahra's sister, Fatimah, who needed more milk. I knew Dr. Dashti came home from work around 4:00, so I waited the next day. I rushed to his car and said, "Zahra needs more milk for her sister, Fatimah. But she can get just one for herself at school. She asked me to register for milk so she could take it for her sister, but I didn't want to.

Can you tell your wife, our headmistress, to give 2 milks to Zahra for Fatimah?"

He said, "Wait, wait, I don't know what you're talking about. Come in."

I was sort of scared of the headmistress and refused to go in. I left feeling as though I had been rude to ask.

A few days later Dr. Dashti told me, "I cannot interfere in my wife's business, but I have milk for you from my office."

So I took two boxes of dried milk and he helped me read directions from the box on how to prepare the milk for a baby. I ran to Zahra's house and gave the boxes to Zahra's mother and said, "Do you know how to make this for Fatimah?"

She didn't, so I showed them how. I did that for a long time for Fatimah and I felt like I was breast feeding her—always anxious to get the milk and bring it on time. I enjoyed that job very much.

It was our separation time when Shazdeh's family came home from vacation in Paris because Mom had to take Ashi back to her place. Ashi could only come to stay with us when the Shazdeh's family was away on vacation, for one month each year in the summer. Sometimes they had another long vacation during the year as well. When Ashi left us she returned to our father's house in a valley in Hasan Abad Square where my father's family lived in other houses close by, and where my father worked. There were about 40 people living in four big houses. Ashi always brought us her memories and told us a lot of stories about life with those families.

Aki and I talked a lot about Ashi's life. This time Aki was very worried about what was going on. I asked her why.

She answered, "Remember when you asked me where babies come from? Ashi later came to me and told me she knew a lot about these things. She learned them from our aunt's husband who is abusing her. She said she witnessed a lot of adult lovemaking."

Aki was scared for Ashi, but told me to keep the secret for myself.

"If Mom knew, she would kill herself," said Aki.

I was very depressed and my heart was squeezed by the whole situation. We all hid our tears, trying to comfort one another by acting strong.

Thank God when Shazdeh's family came home from vacation. They had lots of parties which meant lots of work for Mom—shopping, cooking and preparation. Mom was very preoccupied with the pain of Ashi's absence, but she didn't have any time to be sad. When Shazdeh's family had parties in the house, Mom refused help from Aki or me because she wanted us to enjoy the party and learn to socialize from the Shazdeh's family. This was a huge sacrifice for her because she could have used our help so much. I realize now that by doing this, she taught me to distance myself from her.

I used to come home from school and go right to our little room. I was alone there until Mom finished work. But today when I came home she was lying on the floor, grabbing a blanket. Her face was pale and she was groaning and writhing in pain. I dropped my school bag and asked what was wrong.

She said, "I'm dying."

From her face, I really believed that I was losing her. I rushed across the road to my headmistress's house where her husband, Dr. Dashti, had his office. My headmistress opened the door and I pushed her back and ran through the house.

"Where is Dr. Dashti? Where is Dr. Dashti?"

The headmistress asked why I was so panicked.

I said, "My mom is dying and I want Dr. Dashti."

I had been sent to get the doctor twice before because Shazdeh was sick. I was always polite at the door and he was ready with his bag. This time I was so panicked I didn't know what I was doing. Dr. Dashti was changing in the bedroom. I went to his room and took his hand.

He asked me to let him change first, but I said, "No, my mom is dying." I pulled him and didn't let him get changed. He wore only a robe and his pants.

He said, "Nobody sees me like this! I am a doctor and you are ruining my reputation."

I brought him to the room beside my Mom.

As soon as he examined her, he said, "You're right, this is a serious matter. She has appendicitis and should be in a hospital right now."

He jumped in the car and rushed her to the hospital. I was wondering if Mom would survive until they operated. At the hospital the doctors said it was very close to bursting and she would have died if we hadn't rushed.

After Dr. Dashti left for the hospital, I went to my room. His cook offered to take me home to play with his children, but I thanked her and said I wanted to be alone.

I rushed to our small room, opened Mom's *janamas* (prayer rug), wrapped her chador around me, and put my head on the *mohr* (prayer stone) that she used. I cried myself to sleep and dreamed of a garden full of white jasmine. I wanted to go towards them but my feet were glued to the floor. There was no power, no energy to go. It was a very mixed-up feeling. I heard a violin sound that touched my heart, and then I saw the willow tree I loved like a grandfather coming toward me. It came very close and put all its shade around me. Everything just started to make me feel very relaxed and calm. Because I was lying on the ground and my face was on the prayer stone, the smell was earthy, combined with the jasmine fragrance. I think that's the meaning of heaven. I had no worries about Aki, Ashi, and my mom—nothing.

The next thing I remember was Shazdeh's daughter, who was also my teacher at school, shaking me. "Don't you want to go to school today? Hurry up, it's late!"

Mom was released from the hospital after a week and came home pale and weak. She started back to work right away. Our neighbors helped and Mom paid them with her salary to come and do work like washing clothes and helping to prepare meals. She really did most of the work herself, even when she hired them to do it. I remember a helper snoring when she was supposed to be outside washing clothes. My mom was doing the wash by herself.

I said, "Mom, the helper is sleeping. This is not helpful to you."

She said, "Everyone gets tired and needs to rest. So let her sleep."

I said, "But you never have time to rest yourself!"

Everyone in the neighborhood loved her.

I felt extremely lonely, insecure and scared after this incident. But on the other hand, when Aki and Ashi came to help we had a very good family gathering. One dream stayed with me—I repeatedly dreamed that my mom fell down and died, and the neighbors all came and took her away, put her in a coffin and raised it on their hands, praying to Allah. Her hands hung out of the coffin, and I tried to reach her but couldn't. I was running after the coffin.

I woke up sweating and my heart was beating very fast. I was relieved, reached for my mom and felt her next to me, then was able to go back to sleep. This was a nightmare for all of my teenage years. I never wanted to go to sleep and have this nightmare again.

ne Friday night Aki came to me and said, "Let's go to a not-invited wedding tonight. We'll invite ourselves. We're not invited, but we are going anyway because it is going to be beautiful, and lots of senators, representatives and famous people will be there. I want to see this and I'll take you with me."

She took me to the small garden pond where we washed ourselves. We took off our dresses and scrubbed ourselves with soap to make us shiny. While we were bathing, Shazdeh's son, Parviz, came walking past the pond.

We suddenly saw him and Aki said, "Cover your private!! Cover your private!!" and we ran into the pond to hide ourselves. He stared, embarrassed, and his face turned strawberry red. Then he turned and rushed away. We both laughed and made fun of him.

We finished washing and got all dressed for this special occa·sion in our room at the bottom of the garden. It was before sunset when Aki told Mom we were going to the wedding next door where the senator's son was getting married.

Because it was a neighbor she told Mom, "You will be able to see the lights and hear the music. We will be safe."

Mom wanted to come pick us up because there were no street lights but Aki said we would be late.

We went behind the garden and the gardener's children helped us sneak under the fence between the back yards without ruining our dresses. My heart was beating so hard. We walked across the garden to join people partying around the pool. There were lots of big, shiny lights projecting upward from the tree bases and strings of small lights decorating the whole yard. An orchestra was playing Persian classical music. That was the first time I actually heard a violin. The music just washed my soul and went through my bloodstream, calming me. All my nervousness was gone. I absorbed the music and it took all my worries away. We found a special place to sit. We were very well mannered and well dressed, so none of the guests knew we were not invited. The gardener's children left us because they didn't fit in, but we sat politely in the glory of the moment. The party was huge—there were more people than I had ever seen in one place. We were very hungry but were afraid to be noticed, so we didn't touch any food. But we still had the best time.

We left about 1 AM, with the guests still going strong. When we got home, Mom was sitting and waiting happily for us. She said that the next day she would go and thank the hosts for this invitation because we did not bring any gift, not even a flower. I don't know whether she ever did but if she knew we had not been invited, she would have punished us for sure. So I think she did not ever go and was just honored that we had been invited.

Another party we attended was for the whole family, some neighbors, and Shazdeh's sisters and brothers. When Dr. Dashti arrived, I said, "Hello." The way he answered me honored me.

"Oh, hi, you hero girl," he said in a loud voice. "This girl came to my house and took me to visit her mother. She didn't even give me time to put my pants on—just rush, rush, rush—and she saved her mom's life." People who heard this admired me, and it was interesting to me that Aki wasn't jealous at all, and looked like she admired me too.

Narges' mom, our neighbor's servant, was at the garden door talking to my mom, inviting us to her daughter's wedding. "You can send your daughters today and please don't forget to come yourself tomorrow morning." Then she left.

Mom said, "Poor Narges, she's only 12 years old. Find Aki and get ready for the *aroci* (wedding)."

The custom was for young girls to attend to the bride on the wedding night, and older women to congratulate and bring gifts to the new "woman" the day after (*patakhti*).

Aki, as always, was obsessed with reading. She always volunteered to go and buy the groceries because they wrapped the food in newspapers and when the food was put away she would have the papers to read. Mom was always angry at her because she never paid attention to anything else.

She was reading a magazine and I grabbed it from her and said, "Let's go, we have to go to Narges' wedding." Aki really wanted to finish that last page and was not letting go, but I was in such a rush to go to the wedding.

I said, "Aki, let's go to the pond to wash ourselves like we did for the other wedding."

She said, "No, this is not the same kind of wedding. We will have the same dress but we don't need to wash so carefully and scrub our faces."

When we dressed up, Aki looked gorgeous with that dark green dress from Mom's trunk, sweet pink skin and her very bright brown curly hair. My hair was very straight—like Mom's. I remember Aki curtsied to me, and I loved that gesture.

"Where did you learn this?"

"Bita always does this." Bita's father was the senator who Narges' mother worked for. I expected this to be just like the big wedding we had attended before. I was looking forward to hearing the violin again, seeing lots of cookies and enjoying the guests.

On the way over, Aki said, "If they offer something for you to eat, the first time say no, the second time say no, and the third time only take a little. This is an Iranian custom called *tarof*—even if you're dying to have something, you turn it down twice." This was a sign of being well-mannered and I had to obey even if I didn't like it. When I asked why, Aki was very annoyed with me.

I asked, "Do you know who Narges' husband will be?"

She said, "Do you remember the clergyman who chants Qur'an in the mosque? You said you always go to the mosque to just listen to the voice that you love, and when you hear it your heart has butterflies."

I said, "Oh, I wish he would marry me! Why is he marrying Narges?"

Aki laughed at me and said, "Oh, you silly. You're only a little girl."

I asked Aki, "Do you want to get married?"

And she said, "No, I want to be a surgeon. You know what kind? A heart surgeon."

And I said, "I want to be a teacher."

We went to the wedding. In place of the festive garden party it was in the servant's one-room quarters at the end of the mansion. There was no orchestra, no men and women dancing together, no three-tiered cake and only about 15 young girls with colorful chadors. It was not at all what I expected.

I said to Aki "We don't have chador."

She said, "Chador are for poor people."

We were waiting for someone to invite us in. I said, "No, Mom has a chador."

She told me, "Mom is poor too."

We took our shoes off and entered the room.

I stared at Narges' face. This wasn't the same Narges that I knew yesterday because her eyebrows were connected yesterday and now they had plucked the middle of her brows. She was in a long white dress. They put lots of makeup and very red lips on her—she looked like a doll to me and I loved her. She had a colorful chador hanging on her seat in case a man came in.

It was just Aki and me in our elegant velvet gowns to the floor, with the top of ribbons and lace with pearl buttons down the front. Because our dresses were so elegant and all the girls were sitting on the floor except the bride, they brought two chairs for us to sit by the bride so we would not ruin our gowns. Everybody stared at us.

So I said, "Where is the groom?"

Narges said in a very soft voice, "They are next door in the neighbor's garden—all the men with the groom."

Aki said "For Gods sake, stop questioning. The bride's not supposed to talk to anybody." So we sat there. And when

I thought about that clergyman, imagining him with Narges, I deeply envied her.

The girls were playing *dayereh* and one by one they danced in front of the bride, pulling one another up to join the dancing. She was humble, shy and down to earth. Each time they danced they put their chador down and showed their pretty, colorful dresses of lace and satin. They always smiled. If one didn't know how to play the drum, someone played for her. It was a very happy time. When each finished, she put the chador back on and sat and then the next one stood up and took a turn. My heart started beating hard. What if they ask us to do the same thing—I didn't know how to do it. But because we seemed very different sitting on the chairs, thank God no one asked us to dance. For me, it was puzzling that in the other wedding the bride and groom were together, hand in hand with everybody together. But here was just a small room with no men around. We had a very good time and then left for home.

The next day I saw my mom wrapping Narges' gift—a big, shiny glass pitcher. I asked to go with Mom, and she said, "Yes, why not? But I'm not going to stay long because I don't have time." Mom took the gift and put on her chador. So then I knew that Aki was right—my mom is poor.

As soon as we arrived at Narges' house, I saw a big difference between yesterday's Narges and today's Narges. She was lying down on a blanket looking very pale, tired and sick. But everybody around her—her mother and aunts—was so happy and laughed and made jokes. The wedding night was the big test of virginity and she had passed. Her mother was so proud.

Then I heard Narges' mom telling my mom with pride, "Oh, you don't know how much blood was on the sheet. It was like cutting a cow's head."

I was so surprised, and asked "From where?"

My mom said, "Shhhhh—it is not your business."

Then one of Narges' relatives made a joke, she said, "From her nose."

Then they told one another not to say anything in front of me because I was a child.

Mom said, "Excuse me. This is a little gift." It is traditional to say that any gift you give is not worthy of the recipient, but just a token.

I didn't understand this yet, and again I couldn't just be quiet so I said, "This is a big pitcher."

Mom whispered in my ear "Don't embarrass me—this is *tarof*—even when it is big you say it is little."

They brought a very special food, *kachi*, for the bride to eat. Made of flour, lots of oil, saffron and rosewater, it was like a cookie and the smell was lovely. *Kachi* is made for special ceremonies like death, birth and having a baby, or any time one needs extra strength. It is believed the taste, smell and calories help the person, and just a little bite gives lots of energy. I loved the taste and smell of that *kachi* but knew even if they offered it, I had to say no. They brought it for Narges, but one of the aunts said to give a little to me because the smell was really tempting. I thanked her but didn't say anything. So they brought part of it on a plate toward me and offered it again.

I thought, 'Oh, my God, I have to say no.'

So I said, "No thanks." I was counting on and dying to have that food. I begged God that they should offer just one more time.

On the third time, I said, "Oh, yes thank you!" and grabbed

it. My mom whispered in my ear that I was embarrassing her very much. The taste of that *kachi* is still with me.

I had a big question mark in my mind and couldn't figure out what had happened. So as soon as we left Narges and went home, I went to find Aki and asked, "Do you know what happened to Narges? He hit her and there was a lot of bleeding."

Aki told me it was bleeding from her private parts, not from hitting. I asked why, but she shushed me and said not to ask why anymore. Through whispers throughout the village, I learned that the groom used a long door handle to take Narges' virginity because he was ashamed that he could not break the membrane of the 12 year old himself. Later I often saw the same case in hospitals with poor village people. And I couldn't believe how someone who had that unforgettably soothing voice could be as cruel as that.

The old, unused mosque wasn't fit to be used any longer and was located in a very wide gathering yard. The whole wall and door were still intact. It was a huge space with a lot of empty rooms for playing 'hide and seek.' Aki and I loved it there. It was a place for children to play and gather. There was a beautiful natural *ghanat* (spring) with water coming up from under the ground. Some people who didn't have running water used to go there to drink and take water home in clay pots. The water was warm in the winter, cold in the summer and very clear and tasty. We sat by the spring and challenged one another to see who could hold their hand in the freezing water longer—we counted. Sometimes I won and sometimes Aki did. There were many white berry trees for natural snacks whenever we wanted. We took Mom's chador and spread it under the tree. Aki climbed up and shook the branches and we brought berries home for the week. The local children were also there, and after school and in the summer we played with them—dodge ball, volley ball, and jump rope. We counted up to 10 and back down again, up to 20 and down, up to 30 and down… until we missed or were too tired to continue. Most of the time Aki was the strongest and was the winner.

Sometimes when a villager died they put the dead body on a wooden bed far from the spring, and then friends and spiritual people helped wash the body with water from the spring. Then they covered the body with a plain white sheet and carried it to the cemetery to bury in a grave. Most people didn't like to see a dead body. For Aki and me it was very interesting to watch and it satisfied our curiosity. If the dead person was a woman there were no men around, and visa versa. We didn't care that some people said we would have nightmares.

One day my mom came in from shopping and said all the local stores were closed because the *kulkhoda* (elder leader and wise man of the community) passed away. So we went out and Aki said she wished she was a boy so she could go see *Katkhoda's* body. The entire time we were walking on the street I was trying to think about how to make Aki's wish come true.

Aki said, "If we had a brother we could wear his hat, coat and pants. Then no one would know we were girls." But we decided to go anyway.

We went to a place near the old mosque to see what was going on. A few people were there and some were carrying a coffin on their shoulders. It is the custom for people to follow at least seven steps behind the coffin. I noticed the small booth where a shoe repairman usually sat and shined shoes. If he wasn't there he put an old black curtain around which meant the shoe repair was closed. I told Aki we could hide there and watch everything. She thought it was a good idea, so we tried it.

The black sheet was old and full of holes so we could see outside. We decided to stay and watch even if it took as long as one day. It seemed like a month until they came to wash the body, but the good thing was that we were close to that wooden bed and could see the body very well. So finally they brought the body and put it on the wooden bed and we could see everything. Because he was such a special man in the community everyone stood far away for respect. They took turns taking the sheet off to put the body in the right position.

The first thing that caught my eye was "He has three of them! Look at his privates!" He was old and his testicles were hanging to the sides—so with his penis in the middle, it seemed like 3! It was so interesting for me—we had no men around.

Aki said, "Shut up! They are going to kill us if they find us!"

It was really like torture not to move, not to eat, not to talk. It seemed to me like a very slow movie that took forever. They prayed and washed the body then covered it with the *cafan* (white linen sheet) tied at both ends. The only interesting time for me was the first moment and then I started to fidget. So we sat on the floor breathing very slowly, squeezing our legs, and I thought I'd like to go to sleep.

They began to move, said some religious words and lifted the body toward the cemetery. Finally they left and it was a great relief for us that we could go home. When we got there I was really, really tired. I put my head on a pillow and was gone.

In the Shia branch of Islam, there is a special religious event in the month of *Muharam*, the days of *Tasua* and *Ashura* that has a national secular feeling. Everyone joins in—rich, poor, Christian, Jewish, Bahai, Zaroastarian—everyone. The holiday celebrates how Holy Imam Hussein, grandson of Prophet Mohammed, sacrificed himself and his family for freedom. I heard a quote from Ghandi that said if you're not a religious person at least you can respect freedom like Imam Hussein did. This holiday celebrates freedom.

In my teenage years my outside personality was very modern and outgoing. Inside me my mother's beliefs were alive. I was deeply spiritual and religious. I prayed and meditated with the flowers and frogs. I had my own celebrations with them. I read the Qur'an and was in love with the chanting. Each time I heard Azan I got goosebumps. I went to the mosque for every ceremony. I always had my chador with me to go to the mosque and my miniskirt underneath to go to a party. I never felt guilty about these two ways and figured this must be the way it is supposed to be.

Shazdeh's house had black flags on the doors and the entrance walls were covered with black curtains to show their sorrow during

Tasua and *Ashura*, the day that Imam Hussein was killed. Men didn't shave their beards for those two days and they wore black shirts. Every woman wore a black chador.

In Shazdeh's home they celebrated thoroughly. They cooked for the poor and there was a microphone in the garden for clergymen to tell the story, pray and make people cry. The door was open for two days and all people were welcomed to the ceremony.

On the day of *Ashura* I was helping Mom serve trays of tea, both of us in black chador. Unlike other parties, she insisted that we should sacrifice our whole time for this ceremony and serve the guests, doing good so God would shower favors on us in return. My job was carrying a light tray with small crystal glasses filled with tea.

I went to serve an elderly clergyman who was wearing an *aba* (black cloak) and *ammameh* (white turban), leading the story of the Imam's sacrifice and how he died. Everyone was crying profusely, some pounding their chests to show their pain. I found myself standing face to face with the clergyman—feeling so honored to be serving tea to this holy man. I had the tray in my hands and his hands went under the tray and chador and he grabbed my breasts. I was shocked.

I pushed the tray up and started yelling, "Oh, God, did you witness what he did to me?" I called my mother but she was very busy.

He made a face like, "What's wrong?"

I said, "You devil, you touched my breasts under my chador."

Then I saw Mom hold her face, saying, "Oh, My God." She took me away.

I heard everyone saying to me, "Shame on you! What are you talking about?" They apologized to the clergyman.

Mom pulled me into the house and asked how I dared to say this to a clergyman. I told her that he really did touch me.

I was crying, "Mom, believe me. He did this to me."

She said, "Who's going to believe you? You should know how to deal with a situation like this. Just ignore it, shut up and run away. Look how everybody's pointing at us! If you hadn't defended yourself like that, no one would know what happened, and your reputation would be clean. I don't know what to do with you. You're a rebel!"

I was embarrassed that I had handled this situation so badly. But more deeply, I was very angry at the clergyman's indecency, and furious at the people who judged me and were indifferent to me. I was especially conflicted about the comparison of this event with the Imam's story. How could they act so holy and yet allow this injustice? This one situation changed my entire spiritual life... it loosened the rope of Islam that had bound me and it freed my soul from the reverence I felt for the Muslim leaders in my life. It has stayed with me forever.

Shazdeh's brother, Taj-Malak, was an intellectual, secular, 70 year old man who read poetry and played sitar. He was our neighbor and the two homes shared adjoining gardens with no fence between them. His villa was smaller than our garden but with the same beauty. His 55 year old wife, whom he loved dearly, became handicapped about five years earlier and was living in a separate portion of the villa with her own servant. They had four grown children living far away. Mom and I liked her very much and went to pray with her. She loved it. Over time we established a relationship.

In conversation, she asked her husband, Taj-Malak, to teach me poetry and sitar. Taj-Malak spent most of his time in his library—smoking, reading and playing the sitar. The room was middle-sized with tree size shelves full of books. One side had a large window facing the garden. Two beautiful arm chairs were there with carpeted cushions. He had an indoor white Persian cat, Emerald, with two big eyes like emeralds and an 18 karat gold collar. I compared this cat to the others around the garden and thought it was very fussy and spoiled rotten.

I used to go to him and use his poetry books by Hafiz, Saadi, Khayyam and Rumi to memorize the poems. He taught me to read the poems while he was playing the sitar, an art style called *Dek-lameh*. I became very good at it in Farsi.

Taj-Malak was very kind but not a religious man. When we read poems together he always argued with me about God, and I always quoted from Mom about what God says. He never attended the *Ashura* ceremony and made fun of Imam Hussein.

So one time he told me, "Ask your mother to bring God down so we all can see him. And if your mom is really a Muslim as you say, then God would come down for her and we will all start to believe. You know what? My God is this cat (pointing to Emerald). My God is music. My God is Dr. Dashti who once saved me when I was dying."

He made me seriously think about God. One time I took this matter to Mom.

She answered, "Next time you see Mr. Taj-Malak, ask him who created those musicians? Those poems? Dr. Dashti? And the cat?" Then she continued, "If you don't see something, it doesn't mean that it doesn't exist. This is the limitation of our sight."

I was confused and stopped asking any more questions.

I used to go there after school but never asked him any more questions. I just wanted him to teach me about poetry and how to play the sitar.

Soon after my incident with the clergyman, I went over to the porch and sat to listen to Taj-Malak's beautiful music. It was almost dark. Then he said he had heard that something happened and wanted to know about it. I was so sad and cried. I told him I believed in religion and the clergyman but I didn't know how he could have done this to me, and that no one would believe me.

He said, "Oh, I believe you. I promise I'll go after that son-of-a-bitch."

He asked me to show him how it happened. "How close were you to him?"

So we both stood up and I got close, but was careful not to get too close. All of a sudden he grabbed me and pulled me to him and put his lips on my lips. The feeling—I think I never liked kissing after that—was like very dirty jelly somebody puts in your mouth. I felt so nauseous and didn't want to swallow my saliva. I tried to push him away.

He said, "Don't panic. I just want to show you the feeling of kissing and take away your sadness. How was that?"

All the saliva I was trying not to swallow I spit in his face, kicked him hard in the crotch, struggled and ran away. "Go away, you old, Godless dog!" I screamed.

Mom washed very dirty pots by scrubbing them with soil from the pond. I took a handful of that soil and washed my lips to try to make them clean. I wished I could have been absorbed by the pond and disappear. I started to hide myself behind poetry books and started being more interested in this secular point of view as an alternative to the religious life I now disdained. I learned from my mom—shut up and run away!

When Ashi was away from us her life was totally different than ours and in the control of others. In the winter, Shazdeh's family was home, so there were extended periods of time when Mom couldn't bring her to stay with us.

In Rasoul's house Ashi made herself busy. Since she didn't go to school, there was no holiday or weekend. Every day was alike.

One day Auntie Esmat came and said, "Oh, let me see, you are a big woman now."

She touched Ashi's breasts as she spoke. "It's time for you to get married."

Ashi hated when Esmat touched her, but Esmat came close and put a gold necklace on Ashi—a chain with jingly coins and earrings to match. She gave her a very cheap, white cotton dress with big red flowers. Ashi was happy and thought they were going somewhere special. Esmat combed Ashi's hair around her neck and shoulders.

Then she exclaimed, "My God, look at you. You're so beautiful!"

Farima arrived and asked where they were going.

Esmat said, "I'm taking Ashi home with me for a week."

Farima warned, "Her father is not here and I don't have his permission."

Esmat retorted, "Don't worry, I have his permission." Then they left.

In Esmat's house, Ashi played with the jewelry but didn't like the dress Esmat had bought her and told her so. Esmat laughed and said, "But I see you're enjoying the gold because you're like your mother. You're in love with jewelry."

Two days later, as Esmat had already planned, she took Ashi out. Esmat was heavy and when she walked she became short of breath. They walked slowly and then took a bus. Ashi was embarrassed by all the attention of strangers toward her jewelry and thought she was so overdressed for that moment. Esmat was covered with a dark blue chador printed with tiny white and yellow flowers. People stared, which made Ashi very uncomfortable. She tried to hide herself behind the chador.

After a short time they got off the bus and started to walk.

Esmat panted and said jokingly, "Hey, give me your hand. I don't care if I lose you, but I don't want to lose my gold if somebody kidnaps you."

Ashi thought how mean she was. "These are my gold pieces now, not hers!"

They reached a small, old, three story building and went up a lot of narrow, dirty, broken steps to the third floor. Although they went slowly, step by step, Auntie Esmat was almost out of breath when they reached an old office. Esmat knocked on the office door.

A tall, skinny man with a huge, bushy moustache greeted Esmat in Azari.

"*Khosh-Gal-dean* (Welcome)."

Esmat answered in Azari.

He invited them inside, and when they entered Ashi rushed to the window. It was so interesting to see the street from that height. A few cars passed by and she saw two horse-drawn carriages carrying people around. Although she was looking outside, she grabbed Esmat's chador, not to be left alone.

The man brought tea for Auntie and looked at Ashi in a way that went through her skin like a needle. A moment after, Esmat's husband, Zakey, and his brother, Yadi, arrived. Yadi was a huge, muscular and tall man with kind eyes but very dirty teeth. He had a trimmed, pencil style moustache, like Clark Gable's. He was a tailor but he was dressed in a baggy-style suit, looking a bit too big and floppy.

Fear came to Ashi's heart, and it started to beat hard. "Oh, my God, what's going on? Maybe I did something wrong and they are going to punish me."

The man brought tea for Yadi and Zakey too. Then a clergyman with a long black cloak and white turban entered. Everybody stood up to greet him. "*Salam Aghaga* (Hello)."

He answered, "*Salam-mon-alakom*" and invited them to sit down.

Ashi momentarily felt better when she saw the clergyman, and then he started to pray loudly, "In the name of God . . . For your own health."

Everyone said "*Al-la-home-ma Sal-leh ala -mohammad -en-va-al-e-mohammad* (Greetings to Mohammad and his family)."

This prayer touched Ashi and made her calm because she remembered Mom always said these words in her prayers. She taught Ashi if she was in trouble, just repeat this five times and you will be out of trouble. So Ashi repeated that chant again and again to herself.

As they sat there Ashi didn't know what they said but the clergyman looked at her kindly and stroked his long, long beard. "*Ham-shireh*, (Sister) your Auntie didn't provide me any written permission from your father, but she has two male witnesses, and I can accept that. Do you agree?"

Ashi didn't know what he was talking about. Auntie Esmat signaled her to say yes with a sneaky look and gesture. She was scared and obeyed immediately. She said "*Ba-leh* (Yes)."

They put her fingerprint along with all the witnesses' fingerprints on the document.

The clergyman announced, "Now you are Mr. Yadi's wife."

Everybody stood up and Auntie's husband kissed the clergyman's hand and passed him some money. Everyone said goodbye and left the building.

When they came to the street Ashi was confused and disoriented. She knew something was terribly wrong and her oversensitive hearing picked up some whispering, but she hoped she was wrong.

Auntie Esmat seemed agitated and tired. She took an envelope to Yadi, the new "groom" and said, "OK, we made a deal. The *Baghe Anar* (Pomegranate Garden) is now mine. Sign and put your fingerprint here and as I promised, Ashi is yours."

Then she turned to Ashi, acted sweetly and said, "*moo-ba-rak -bashe -aroos Khanoom* (Congratulations, new bride)." And she started to unclasp the necklace and bracelet and took the earrings saying, "Oh, my darling, you're so young to have these. I will take care of them."

"No, no!" Ashi said as she tried to stop her.

Esmat struggled with Ashi aggressively until Ashi let go of the jewelry and gave up fighting. She felt so lonely and just wanted Mom. She cried for Rasoul to come and save her.

Then Auntie Esmat and her husband said, "Goodbye" and started to walk away.

Yadi offered his hand for Ashi to go with him.

Ashi grabbed Esmat's chador and screamed like crazy, "No, No, I don't want to go with him. Don't leave me."

Her screams attracted people's attention all around. Bothered and embarrassed, Esmat said "Oh, you devil. OK, let's go."

It is summer and all the doors are open. At 9 PM, Shazdeh's family relaxes inside and listens to classical music on the radio. It is comfortably cool so everyone enjoys the clean, pure air, permeated with the smell of jasmine.

The Qajar indoor world is totally different from mine. Their mansion is in a small town north of Tehran, Shemiron, which has very dark nights and not many street lights. Inside there are diffused, calming lights. When the music starts, as they lie down to listen, I lie down in the garden on a wooden bed covered with a Persian silk rug in a sheer tent of mosquito netting. Everyone uses this bed when they rest outside. Nobody inside knows I am there listening and how much that music touches my heart, my soul—like life blood coursing through my veins. I wait all day for that moment.

The wooden bed, though elegant and sophisticated, does not comfort me as much as lying outside the tent directly on the ground so I can see the unfiltered sky, moon and stars and feel the soil sift through my fingers. I love that feeling. The willow tree is there—my grandfather; and the jasmine; ground and sky surround and support me. I feel unfulfilled until the smells of jasmine and soil awaken my senses. The darkness of night makes such a wonderful world for me.

I look up at the beautiful, dark-blue velvet sky with many bright stars, then turn to the pond, seeing the reflection of that larger world in the water's surface. I notice the stars are mirrored by the tadpoles' movements in the water and the reflection of the moon creating two skies. Maybe the music brings the stars down to the pond, I think, and they change into tadpoles. The smell of jasmine is all around the tent, and between the two skies I am lifted into a free world on an almost imperceptible breeze. The nighttime stars transform into a flowing handkerchief dancing in the sky…star…Setareh…dancing handkerchief…I drift off to sleep.

I dream that the biggest star is Grandma, descending toward a huge willow tree. The tree, Grandfather, reaches out his branches to her. I stand between them, dancing with the sweet handkerchief—connecting my family roots. She comes very close to the tree and then disappears. The handkerchief falls and I rush to grab it. I'll never forget the feeling of my Grandmother and Grandfather hugging me at the same time, wrapping me with nurturing protection that washes away my loneliness.

My sweet dream is interrupted by Mom's worried voice. She shakes me awake. "It's so late! What are you doing out here? I was worried when I didn't find you in our room and called you over and over again."

I don't want to come out of that dream. I tell Mom about my dream and she gives me an alarming but knowing look. She shows me the framed handkerchief, saved in her trunk.

ur aunt, Esmat, Rasoul's sister, grabbed Ashi's hand and they all started to walk. Four blocks away they reached a big square house with no trees or green at all.

Inside the courtyard were 12 doors, each for one room. There was a small pond at the middle of the yard for washing clothes and dishes. The doors were all scratched and dirty. Yadi opened the lock to one of the rooms and they went inside. It had an old rug on the floor and the room smelled moldy. Ashi didn't let go of her aunt's chador. It gave her a lot of security and she wanted to hide herself in the chador forever. Yadi went in the corner of the room to a *cheragh-nafti* (portable oil stove) and made tea. He put three small, glass cups on the tray, and then aunt gave everyone a sugar cube.

She laughed and said, "Here. This is the sweetness to toast the new bride."

She wanted to say goodbye but Ashi didn't want to let her go. Her husband lit a cigarette and went outside. Aunt looked at the reflection of her necklace and earrings in the window—how ugly they were in Ashi's eyes now.

She looked at Ashi and said, "Honey, I have to go. You're

Yadi's wife now—stay with him and start your own life. This is your house now."

Ashi was screaming and pulling herself towards Aunt Esmat. Yadi and Esmat looked at each other and aunt said, "OK we can sit for a while, but that's it."

So Ashi put her head on Auntie's lap, holding her chador, and went to sleep.

Big hands were traveling around her body. Heavy breathing was bothering her ear. She didn't know where she was. Yadi was trying to take her clothes off. It was extremely dark—she couldn't see anywhere. Then she recognized Yadi's voice. "Oh, my beautiful wife—relax. You're like a deer ready to run away. I don't know what to do with you."

She jumped and sat up and said, "I want my aunt. I want my mom. No, I want my dad."

He grabbed her angrily and said, "Enough is enough. You belong to me now. You are my wife and this is our home. What do you want from me? What more can I do?"

Ashi rubbed her eyes, not knowing if this was a nightmare or real. She even missed Farima, her stepmother, and wanted her to come and save her. Ashi pinched Yadi's chest and started to bite him and pull his hair. He laughed and his breath smelled awful.

He said, "You feel very strong. You are really wild! Hit me." Ashi hit him hard, and was trapped in his arms and he held her very tight.

He said, "Don't act childish." Then he put his hand on Ashi's mouth and said, "I don't think this is something new for you."

And he raped her. It was sharp and painful and she felt it into her bones.

The day after as darkness was leaving, Ashi thought "I'm not going to move and I'll pretend I'm sleeping." Then when she heard his deep breathing, she moved a little bit toward the door.

All of a sudden he grabbed her from the back by her long hair, which was very painful. He pulled Ashi toward the closet in the room. He took out a big butcher knife and showed it to Ashi and sneered, "Look at this. If you go, this is your punishment. I'm not joking—this is real. Now you are my wife and I have to show that I have power over you. Otherwise I am not a man. I'm not a man if you leave the house."

The old saying is right that all women are superficial. They are without wisdom. Women are created from only one rib of a man. He kept Ashi in that room for one week, raping and sodomizing her over and over. He left after a week to go to work and gave the key to an old neighbor woman. Ashi watched out the window and learned that this house had a lot of rooms rented to different families. In the center was a big, dry courtyard, two restrooms at the corner—one for men, one for women—and kids were playing barefoot and swearing at each other like crazy. She missed Shazdeh's place with all the trees and flowers. She was so lonely.

"Where are you, Mom?" Ashi called.

She had cried so much she couldn't cry anymore.

Time went so slowly for her. She hated the night; she didn't want the sun to go down. From her windows she saw women talking to each other, making jokes and washing their clothes in a cement tub and hanging them up to dry. Each time she wanted to go to the bathroom she had to knock on the window so one of the women would call the neighbor to come take her out, then return her back and lock the door. Ashi was in prison with no crime. It was almost 10 days and she wondered why these women were not afraid of butcher knives. How could they be outside? How come, with this kind of life, they are laughing and making jokes?" Now Ashi became a housewife.

I escape to my Garden and lean behind the willow tree, eyes closed and half dreaming, remembering when Ashi asked Mom, "What is the meaning of marriage?"

Mom says, "Marriage means men and women complete each other.
They get married and they must stay together for ever."

Then she tells us a story from the Messenger's book.
That day she reads,

"You were born together, and together you shall be forevermore.
You shall be together when white wings of death scatter
        your days.
Aye, you shall be together even in the silent memory of God.
But let there be spaces in your togetherness,
And let the winds of the heavens dance between you.
Love one another but make not a bond of love:

Let it rather be a moving sea between the shores of your souls.
Fill each other's cup but drink not from one cup.
Give one another of your bread but eat not from the same loaf.
Sing and dance together and be joyous, but let each one of you
        be alone,

Even as the strings of a lute are alone though they quiver with
the same music.
Give your hearts, but not into each other's keeping.
For only the hand of Life can contain your hearts.
And stand together, yet not too near together:
For the pillars of the temple stand apart,
And the oak tree and the cypress grow not in each other's
shadow."
—*Kahlil Gibran*

The gardener approaches and washes the willow tree with a long hose and I feel the mist from around the tree gently waking me. I become all wet, then escape to my room, thinking of Ashi's dreams dashed by our father's family.

Shazdeh had another party to socialize with rich and famous friends. There were representatives from the *Majles* (parliament), government ministers and other Shazdehs.

Before the party I heard one of the other gardeners, Mash-Reza, speaking to one of Shazdeh's servants, complaining about how badly he needed money. He had 8 children and his wife had cancer. He said if his wife died he didn't know what to do with the children. He needed to take her for an operation. The servant asked if he had spoken to Dr. Dashti. He said yes, but Dr. Dashti worked only for a pediatric hospital and couldn't help. He was very sad.

I told Aki this story and she said she would write the story down, then we would give the letter to Gilda's father, who was the minister of the health department. We found out that Gilda's father was going to be at the party, so we prepared the letter to give to him.

At the party, Aki and I were standing with the letter. All the guests arrived and when Gilda's father came in, we went toward him with the letter in our hand. Shazdeh saw us and stopped us with a fierce stare. He called us aside with a wave of his hand.

He said, "What do you have in your hand?"

Aki said, "This is for Mash Reza's wife who needs help from the health department."

He said, "This is a party for relaxation and fun. You're not a social worker and this is not an office. Leave him alone and don't bother him."

He tore up the letter, and said not to come to the party because we would embarrass him. Then he groaned, "Mash-Reza. Who cares? How many people do I have to take care of like that?"

Aki and I left the party feeling humiliated and guilty, and not well-mannered. I didn't blame Shazdeh at the time. I thought we were extremely wrong. But Aki was swearing, "The son of a bitch, and selfish air-head! Yesterday he was trying to touch my hand and I pinched him. The mark is still on his hand. The old bastard!"

Mash-Reza's wife died within a few months. We couldn't play that day because of the deep sorrow in our heart for his children who we had played with so often.

It was another summer vacation time and Mom went to bring Ashi home. She couldn't find Ashi at my father's place. She looked in every house in Hasan-Abad valley for her and through the neighbors, found out about Ashi's new life. Then she desperately went to her brother, Latif, and explained the situation to him. She begged him for help. The same day, together, they went to the police and asked for legal intervention.

All of a sudden Ashi saw Mom and her brother, Latif, coming with a policeman. Yadi was following them.

They came toward the door and Ashi screamed "Oh, God." Again she rubbed her eyes. "Am I dreaming?"

Mom jumped in, "Oh, my poor baby. Oh, my beautiful gem! What are you doing here? When is the end of all of this pain?" She was pointing to the sky, "God, are you there? Are you witnessing this? Where is Rasoul? Is he a man or a back stabber—an evil bastard traitor? Is this the way a father should treat his 13 year old child?"

Then she pointed at Yadi, "Shame on you! Look at you! You are my age! You are a loser son of a bitch! How dare you do this to us? I will pursue you. I will send you to jail for this abduction."

Mom went to Ashi and wrapped her arms around her and stayed there motionless.

Ashi grabbed Mom and burst into tears. Uncle Latif, the policeman and Yadi argued and showed each other papers.

Then Yadi, with respect, brought the papers to my mom. "Look, I didn't do anything wrong. These are legal papers. I legally married her."

Mom grabbed them "What papers? Are you a man? I don't believe it. You are just an abductor, a child molester. I hate you!"

Yadi left Mom, grabbed the knife from his trouser pocket and went to the middle of the yard. He took off his shirt and pointed the knife at his heart, shouting, "Help! Help! They are taking my wife away!" Neighbors, until now watching from their doors, surprisingly came to his help.

He pointed out the policeman and said, "They bribed him to take my wife away from me! I'm going to cut my heart out."

They grabbed his hands and took the knife away, calming him down. The policeman saw the official papers and ran away. He didn't want to be involved. My uncle started to examine and read the official papers.

He told Mom, "He is right, her father 'gave her away.' These documents show they were legally married!"

In the eyes of the neighbors, Yadi was a victim.

They whispered, "Oh, this poor old guy who we have known for years—he couldn't be an abductor! Such a shame!"

Mom was thinking how she could handle this terrible situation. She desperately asked Yadi if she could take Ashi with her for just one week and promised to bring her back. Yadi agreed. Mom thought that during this time she could find a way to save Ashi from this awful marriage.

Mom left with Ashi, and with her brother, started to fight back right away. Although my uncle searched feverishly, they failed to reach any solution. Mom even tried to get my betraying father's help, but he was a fugitive himself and refused to get involved. Yadi remained supported by the law as a husband. Even the law officer warned Mom that Yadi could complain and go after Mom for harassment, so she was better off to give up and stop, or she would be jailed for fighting against the law.

In Iran, as in many countries, the law protects the man and discriminates against women. Ashi was just one of many innocent children who have been victims of the illegal laws that allow men to dominate and assert their will. Mom gave every piece of herself to save Ashi—finally she surrendered.

I was sitting in our little room at the end of the garden and Aki was playing "math teacher." She was like a private teacher in our neighborhood, teaching math to everyone. She and I were alone because Mom didn't have time off. Mom had one day off each month—when her stepmother came to deliver her small inheritance.

We called Mom's stepmother, Bibi, *Khanoom*, instead of Grandma—just one step less than Your Majesty. That was the level of respect my mom required that we give her. Aki and I were angry that Mom forced us to respect this lady like a queen when she disrespected us, treating us like two homeless bastards. Behind her back we called her *Kaff-tar* (Lady Hyena), because she was Mom's blood sucker.

When my father escaped and took Mom's money, Mom gave her inheritance to Bibi in a sort of trust fund. This kept the money safe as the family transitioned from Ardebil to Tehran. One month, Bibi came in and she and Mom talked for a while. Then she gave Mom her share of the money.

I was still pretending to study my mathematics but was listening to everything. Aki was trying to teach me but I was very preoccupied. I was supersensitive and extremely alert to everything going on around me—the words, feelings and sounds. I could hear even a whisper, and I was very sensitive to smell as well. In any situation, I was aware even when I pretended not to be.

Mom said, "The little bit of money you gave me is not enough. I don't have enough to buy food and clothes. God knows I am working here from 4 am to midnight, and I don't have enough money to do for my children. This money that you gave me is really nothing compared with my father's wealth."

Bibi rolled her eyes like a devil and hollered, "Didn't I tell you to leave the kids with their damn father and come live with us? You are a stubborn woman. You decided to be a servant and ruin our family's dignity and our famous name because of your children. And now you have to pay for that. Didn't I tell you?"

Mom started to cry and Aki rushed to her side.

Mom said, "See what happened to Ashi when I left her with her father? You want me to do the same thing with these two little angels?" And she pointed to us.

Bibi said, "You had the choice of a foster home."

Mom yelled, "Please stop blaming me. Would you put your own children in a foster home?"

Bibi said, "No, because they have their own father's money to live with."

Mom sobbed, "He was my father also."

Bibi retorted, "He was your father, not theirs. That's why we always welcome you but not them. And the money is for you, not for your children."

Mom took some papers out of the trunk and showed Bibi that she had rented the bath in Ardebil, and asked for the document for the bath so she could sell it to save her children. So Bibi went to the trunk to look for more papers, and when they continued this conversation Mom started to calm Bibi down, saying she should take it easy because she had a heart problem.

"I'll make *gool-gov-zaban* (tea) for you to help you relax."

I was always so angry when Mom was kind to Bibi, like she was an innocent lady. I punched Aki's arm and we went outside.

Aki said, "Isn't she the devil?"

I replied, "She is very bad. She doesn't want us at all. She wants us to be out of our mother's life."

Then I said, "Aki, I know how to punish her using one of my students."

Aki said, "Your students?"

I always played in a very big pond with thousands of frogs. That was my private school, from preschool to high school. In my imagination, Aki was the headmaster and I was the principal. Aki laughed.

I said, "Look, we can choose the big one to punish her."

Aki said, "That's a good idea. Do they listen to you?"

So I caught the biggest one. It was very natural for me to touch the frogs. Aki was surprised I was so comfortable with them, but was concerned that I would get warts. Sometimes I took my socks off to cover my hands so the fish and frogs wouldn't feel so slippery.

It was a custom that anyone who came into our room took off their shoes, placed them behind the door and then came in. Out of respect for the guest we turned the shoes around to be ready for leaving.

Aki asked, "What do you want to do?"

I said we would put a frog in the stepmother's shoe. When she puts the shoe on she will faint.

Aki was very happy and said, "Aren't you a genius? I'll go inside and when I come out that means she is ready to leave and you should bring the frog and put it in her shoe."

So Aki went inside and I caught my largest frog. I thought the smallest might get hurt. I apologized to the frog, but said it would only be a short time in a small smelly place, and it should escape at soon as it could. I told the frog that the headmaster would be very happy. The frog made a sound and I was sure this was approval to do this important job for me. So Aki came out, and I had the frog under my shirt because the gardener was watching me curiously to see what I was up to this time.

When the adults said goodbye, my mom was wiping her eyes. I put the frog in the shoe, and stepped back. As soon as Bibi put her foot in the shoe, the frog jumped out. She screamed, and then she fainted (I think she pretended). Mom was scared, and looked for holy water that she always used for healing. Holy water, hysteria, and Bibi watching Aki!

She said "I knew you were going to do something to me, the way you were looking at me."

Aki and I ran to the pond with the frog. Aki and I were screaming, fainting, laughing and jumping like the frog. When we put it down the frog looked very dizzy and was jumping quickly.

I think it was a relief for me to deal with Mom's sadness and anxiety this way. I was always thinking that I could perhaps relieve her pain somehow. After Bibi left, Mom collected the papers to go back in the trunk. All of a sudden we heard a deep scream from her throat. "All the jewelry is gone!" That night we went to the police.

She tried to explain in broken Farsi, but the police made fun of her language and said that she had no proof, so they could not follow up. My mother's dear jewelry was gone.

om brought Ashi home for three weeks to recover from her abduction, before returning her to Yadi. Ashi was 13 years old. We were all playing in the garden. Aki, 15, was talking to Bita, her friend, while Ashi played by the pond. I was 11 years old, and was very interested in the conversation between Aki and Bita. Vida, Bita's older half-sister, was visiting from the United States. Bita's father married an American woman while he was studying in the United States. When he returned to Iran with Vida, (Vida was 10 years old) his wife divorced him. Vida finished high school in Iran, and then went to the United States for college. She came to Iran every summer to visit her father. Bita was ecstatic that Vida was visiting; she always brought her gifts. Bita looked very casual sitting in her new jeans on the grass. All the time they were talking I was paying attention to those jeans and wishing that I had a pair. I got tired of listening, and went to play with Ashi.

Ashi knew that the frogs were my students, and that Aki was the headmaster. Ashi had insisted that she be named the headmaster so she could punish them any way she wanted. And when I saw her, she was killing all the tadpoles. She had a colander in her hand, had pulled all the baby frogs from the water, put them on the ground and squished them with her feet. By the time I arrived only one big frog was stuck in the colander.

I screamed loudly, "No, what are you doing to my frogs?" I sat on the ground and started to cry, and asked, "Why are you doing this? Didn't I tell you they were my students?" It was like a battlefield again.

Aki and her friends heard my scream and came over. In their opinion, I overreacted. Bita said, "These aren't people after all, just frogs!"

Then Aki said, "You two have no tolerance for each other, even for a week!"

Vida came toward me, and she tried to lift me from the ground. She hugged and kissed me, took me on the steps, sat by me and said, "I understand you. I know how difficult this is because you liked those frogs, didn't you?"

I said, "Yes, they were my students, and Ashi killed all of them."

She said, "Yes, but you saved the big frog, didn't you?"

Then Vida said, "Do you know why Ashi did that? Did you say something to make Ashi angry?"

I said, "Ashi is mad because I made Aki headmaster of the Frog School."

Then Vida tried to reach Ashi to talk to her, also stroking her head and speaking calmly to her, asking the same question, "Why did you do that?"

Ashi started to cry very hard and did not say anything.

I think that day I was introduced to American culture through Vida's kindness, understanding and extreme care for people's feelings. Although she wasn't American, her time in the United States had changed her—she was genuinely open-minded because of her travels. She was very calm and relaxed, different from any of us. For me, this opened a door to seeing the world—it is the first time I imagined a larger world than the one I knew.

Malak-Banoo, the Shazdeh's daughter, was tiny and beautiful with deer-like, kind, black eyes. Her skin was tan and her hair was long to her belt, curly and ebony black. Everyone in her family was worried about how picky she was, and why she hadn't chosen someone already. Finally she chose a very handsome, highly educated engineer, the same age as she was. She got married when she was 29 years old.

The ceremony took place in an elegant club beside Tehran University called *Bash-ghahe-Daneshghah*. Aki and I were wearing our beautiful dresses from Mom's trunk. The club was full of flowers, lights and live music. Kids were all playing, sneaking extra sweets from the tables and crawling underneath to eat. Aki and I were just watching, absorbing the whole scene as outsiders and not joining the other children. We felt like we were in a dream.

At this wedding I learned many social behaviors that were different than in the village where we lived. I learned about the tango and waltz, how ladies always came first and that gentlemen opened doors for them. I learned that you can yawn with a closed mouth and be very careful about every movement you make. You

have to put a napkin on your lap when you're sitting. You can't put
your arm on the table when you're eating. Take very small bites. Use
a knife and fork rather than spoon and fork. And don't talk while
you're eating. This was opposite from the village, where anytime
someone yawned there was a big noisy sigh, or when they ate they
talked with full mouths. In the village, the men walked three steps
ahead of the women. When they called the woman, they said the
first son's name, for example: *mather e Hassan* (Hassan's mother)
rather than her name, Fatima. And I noticed that the guests who
didn't know us thought we were probably bridesmaids and those
who knew us were snobby and wondered why we were there.

Mom had on a plain long black dress with a big white shawl.
She had very beautiful, worried eyes. She knew that this was all
superficial, and we were playing roles like in a movie. We really
didn't belong. Each time I watched her, she was hiding behind
the guests. When I reached her, she encouraged me to enjoy the
guests, not stand by her. That is when I learned to put distance
between us in public.

At the end of the party a long line of cars with beeping horns
and bright, shiny lights wove their way down Palavi Avenue (now
Valiasr Street), to the north. Palavi is famous for the old trees on
both sides, arching over the broad road. It is the longest street
in the Middle East, and perhaps the world. Its 12 miles connect
south and north Tehran. The bride and groom had a new house in
Tajrish-Shemiron. The guests' cars paraded behind the bride and
groom's white Cadillac to their home. All said goodbye, and left.
Aki and I were happy because Malak-Banoo honored us when
she asked us to ride in her car, and I'll never forget that feeling of
closeness and kindness.

Mom had left earlier to manage the welcoming of the bride and groom in their new home. Mom arranged for Malak-Banoo to have a new servant named Tahereh, who was Mom's bread maker's daughter in Ardebil. Tahereh was a happy, funny, fat widow the same age as Malak-Banoo. She made my mom laugh because she was so fat, each time she coughed she farted too, and then she laughed like crazy. I never heard Mom laugh aloud, and she thought that the best mannered people only smiled and controlled their laughter. She tried to teach this to Tahereh and us, but Tahereh was wise enough to ignore her advice. We, however, learned self control from Mom. Tahereh used her laughter to hide the overwhelming sadness of her young husband's death, and the fact she had given her two boys to the orphanage so she could work and survive. When Mom selected Tahereh, she helped her start a new life.

That night, when we came to the house, Mom and the servants were already preparing for the bride and groom to arrive. Mom came to Malak-Banoo, hugged and kissed her like she was leaving her own daughter, and said, "I'm going to miss you like crazy. I'm not going to be with you any more." Malak-Banoo had no mother or sister, and hugged Mom back like her own mother.

Malak-Banoo asked, "Can Mahi stay with me tonight?"

I felt Malak-Banoo's loneliness and fear, and that she needed a little sister to accompany her on her special night. Mom agreed, and left with Aki, who looked very sad leaving me behind.

The groom came and swept Malak-Banoo to their suite, and Tahereh took me to her small room at the end of the house. I couldn't sleep because of Tahereh's snoring, farting and gas—she had too many cookies that night. I was staring at the ceiling and thinking of Narges' wedding. I thought Malak-Banoo would have a terrible night and I would see her very pale and weak the next morning. I thought about the bloody sheet that Narges' mother showed. So most of the night I was awake imagining what was happening in their room. Tahereh was snoring like a bear. I didn't sleep at all that night.

In the morning we left Tahereh's room to go up for breakfast. I saw Malak-Banoo in a white satin robe with fur slippers, beautiful with wet hair on her shoulders and with light makeup left from the night before.

She was happily welcoming me and said, "You looked very beautiful last night."

I flushed with embarrassment. Tahereh was preparing the table for breakfast, and Malak-Banoo asked her to set a place for me too. That touched me. Davood came out with a beautiful, dark maroon silk robe and matching pants. He smelled of cologne. Oh my God, the difference between Narges' wedding morning and Malak-Banoo's. There was milk, honey, eggs in gold egg holders, and matching cups, delicate and beautiful, all on the round table covered with a maroon tablecloth with beige lace over it. The fresh smell of bread permeated the air. There were flowers all around from the night before, and there were two matching China teapots on the table. Davood poured tea for me first and then kissed Malak-Banoo. So I was sitting at the table, enjoying, and comparing Narges' and Malak-Banoo's lives. I wondered how Tahereh worked so fast without farting.

The next day Mom came in with the other guests, bringing gifts and congratulations for the bride and groom. Mom always had a long dress and matching shawl covering her hair, and she looked like a lady. Mom kissed Malak-Banoo and presented an empty, antique jewelry box. This box had once held Mom's jewelry, a gift from her father, all of which had been stolen by Lady Hyena.

Mom said, "I know this is nothing to you, but it is very dear to me." By giving away that box, Mom finished unfinished business, getting rid of everything that was a reminder of her lost jewelry, so she wouldn't care any more.

Malak-Banoo opened the box and said, "This is a beautiful antique piece."

Mom answered, "Yes, my father brought this from Russia for me 40 years ago. And now I am happy that it belongs to you." I was embarrassed that Mom gave Narges a big pitcher, but gave Malak-Banoo a tiny box. I didn't understand that value is about quality, not quantity.

Malak-Banoo's house became my second home. Malak-Banoo made me feel like a princess during and after her wedding, becoming more of a friend than a teacher. She had a television, and it was great fun to stay with her and watch it, even though TV was only programmed until 10 PM (sometimes 12). I watched John Wayne movies. In one of them he found gold, and I got the idea that America was a place where you could go and simply find gold. Later on, when I finally got to the United States, I was amazed that John Wayne didn't speak Farsi anymore. It was sweet for me to hear the movies in Farsi, and I have never enjoyed cowboy movies quite as much in English.

I was playing hopscotch outside with my oldest sister, Aki, when a young neighbor man came out of his house. He said, "Hi."

He came towards me and brushed my hair with his hand and then kissed my cheek.

Aki slapped him hard and said, "Never, ever touch my sister again."

He was so surprised. There was no sexual gesture in what he did, but this was a lesson, so whenever he saw me he went to the other side of the road.

I asked her why she did that. "Don't you think he is like a father to us?" I said.

She replied, "We need no father, no brother, and no man in our lives. We will take care of ourselves."

It gave me a good feeling that I had this powerful sister beside me.

Aki was becoming a woman. Her breasts were growing, her hair getting longer and she was very attractive and strong, physically and emotionally. I learned this through the attention the neighborhood men paid to her; many were interested in marrying her. She was also a very talented student, especially in science and mathematics. She read everything in sight—really everything—even the newspaper wrappings from the grocery store. When Mom wanted help, she was always reading. We learned later that her IQ was over 180.

I tried to copy Aki all the time, step by step. She always protected me, taking on the role of a father figure. I was tiny and sensitive; even a look could make me cry. My mom always defended the other people, suggesting that if we were upset it was our own fault somehow.

One day at school, a girl and I started to fight and she kicked me. Of course, I started to cry. Aki found a rope and tied that girl to a tree far from our classes. When the girl was absent from class the teacher looked for her. A schoolmate found the girl and untied her, sending her back to class. She told the story, and Aki was punished by having to wear a big sign on her back, "I am a bad girl." She had to go from class to class. She was so relaxed and chuckling as she went. She came to my class, and made a signal to zip my lip and say nothing. They were going to put a sign on my back too, but Aki took my turn as well as her own. She wore the sign all week, but she really didn't care. For me, that was a great moment, because she protected me heroically, and wasn't affected in the least. She looked happy, and I didn't feel bad for her.

As Aki bloomed like a flower, the older son of the Qajar family, Parviz (his name was the same as my dead brother), fell in love with her. He was a handsome, 22-year-old shy man. He had just graduated from Tehran University, and by law went into the draft. He received a free education in exchange for serving his country. He liked our family very much from the beginning, and treated my mother as a surrogate mom. In some ways, he was also a surrogate for the son she had lost. He totally understood Mom's circumstances and was sympathetic toward us. Mom embraced his spirit.

Knowing that he was in love with Aki, he wrote a letter to Mom letting her know that he was interested in marrying my sister, but unfortunately was trapped and unable to announce his desire. It was not accepted in Iranian culture for a young, educated rich man to marry a poor girl, especially a man from a famous family like his. Mom still believed Parviz would be our salvation and marry Aki. Aki told me that she was in love with Parviz too.

Accidentally Parviz' father intercepted a second letter from him to Mom when it was delivered by the mailman, and therefore became aware of his son's love for Aki. The house was in the fire of anger.

Shazdeh was screaming and yelling at my mom, "Why did you let this happen? You are not a loyal servant! You are just using us! You are taking advantage of us by deceiving my son to save your life."

Mom answered, "No, I swear on the Qur'an that I did not plan this. This is pure feelings sent from God to two beautiful hearts. I'll always celebrate that. God is witness that I did not plan this. It is all God's will."

To avoid this relationship, Shazdeh fired Mom. He told her if she got rid of Aki, maybe she could have her job back.

Mom was desperate, heartbroken and hurt, struggling to figure out what to do with a 14 year old child, and letting go of her dream of Parviz as a son-in-law and savior. She left Shazdeh's house and went to her stepmother, Bibi, hoping that Parviz would come after Aki and save our family. But the Qajar family members were notorious cowards, and Parviz was one of them. He never came to solve this problem.

Mom started a very tough life in her stepmother's house. We knew from the beginning that Bibi couldn't be trusted, and her concern was not for us. Bibi had a plan to keep me and Mom, and get rid of Aki as soon as possible. It was less than a month after we arrived there when she found a 52 year old judge to marry Aki.

Bibi said, "The man is my neighbor, and a very honorable court judge. His wife died about a year ago, leaving him with children 15, 20, and 22. He wants to marry again. So I introduced Aki to him."

Bibi convinced the judge that Aki was not a good student and wanted to run away. She told him Aki would be a great wife because she was so beautiful ("hot and exciting") and he would be helping out our poor mom. She also forced Mom to accept this "deal" for the good of me and herself. Mom told her that Aki was one year younger than his youngest child, and that this was not an appropriate match.

Bibi argued back, "He's going to support Aki, and he's an educated man. You're going to have peace of mind about Aki's future."

Mom felt helpless and discussed this with our uncle, who strongly disagreed with this offer.

Aki heard my uncle tell Bibi, "This is a disaster! What are you doing? You want to ruin Aki's life?"

Bibi somehow convinced him that this was protecting Aki from a worse fate, and he finally acquiesced.

I remembered how much Aki cried, and rejected this idea, saying that she would kill herself. Aki didn't have any concept about married life. She was only worried whether she would have enough time to read newspapers and books. And what about school, would she be able to go?

Then Bibi, in her deceptive way, told Aki that the judge was a rich man and had a servant, so Aki would have all the time she wanted to study and read books. Like a moth to the flame, that convinced Aki to marry the judge.

Finally, Bibi convinced everyone that this was a good idea and her plan was set in action. She planned the whole thing. The marriage ceremony was very private and documented in *amahzar* (law office). In attendance were Aki, the judge, Bibi, Mom, two of Bibi's male relatives as witnesses, and me. Then she held a party at her house, dressed Aki up in that emerald dress from Mom's trunk, and quickly sent the bride and groom home. Aki was gone. Half of me was gone.

Mom was shocked and desperate. She asked herself whether she had done the right thing. She didn't have any patience for me and continually told me to go away. Mom was so angry that she wasn't speaking to anyone, and she told me she was looking for a job so we could leave as soon as possible.

In the judge's house, Aki adapted very quickly, because the

judge's house had everything she needed—a library, kids to play with, and lots of space all handed to her on a silver platter. She felt she owned all of it. The first night the judge didn't bother her at all. He was tired from the party. The second day, Aki had lunch with the judge's family.

Then she asked, "Where is my room?" She loved the judge's daughter, and thought it would be a good idea to share her room. However, they showed her the master bedroom with a bed to share with the judge. The judge came in and Aki asked him if Zohreh his daughter and she could stay in the master bedroom.

The judge thought a little and said, "You're my wife now, and we have to share the room together."

Aki said, "I know I'm your wife, but Bibi told me I will be free to do whatever I want here. So now I want to be with Zohreh, not you."

The judge was a nice man, but didn't know what to do.

He called his daughter, and asked her, "Do you want to take Aki as a guest tonight to your room?"

She happily accepted and took Aki to her room, and they had a lot of fun talking about their past, including both of their moms—and they fell asleep.

On the third day after dinner, the judge sent the kids out, so it was just Aki and him. And again he talked about how a man and woman make a husband and wife, and what must happen. This just went on and on, and Aki was so innocent, all the time speaking to the judge like the father she never had. She thought getting married would make her secure, with a wonderful father.

The judge eventually knew that Bibi had deceived him, and Aki was not the girl she had described. He couldn't believe it himself, and felt trapped in an unethical situation. After one month trying to convince Aki, he realized that although he wanted this marriage, it was a big mistake. So he invited Mom to his house and explained everything.

He said, "Your daughter is so innocent like an angel, and it's too soon for her to get married. Each time I went to her it was like a rape. I must divorce her, because this is not *hallal* for me, a Muslim man of honor. I never touched her. So please take back your virgin daughter, because it is a sin for me to touch this pure innocence. And, by the way, never ever trust your stepmother again. She wants to destroy you."

And when Mom asked for more details, he said, "I'm a judge, and can't say any more than this."

Mom went crazy in the judge's house. For her, this was a disaster.

"What am I going to do? What am I going to say to the neighbors? My stepmother? How am I going to handle this 14-year old virgin divorcee? What future suitor is going to believe in her purity? This will be a scandal!"

She cried out, "Hey God, are you there? I think you must be dead, rather than witness this. What life are you planning for me? What more can you take from me?" She was pulling her hair, and hitting herself.

Aki and I were embarrassed that she behaved this way in front of the judge. The judge tried to calm her down, brought her a *sharbat*((sweet drink with rosewater), and knelt in front of her.

He took her hands and said, "You are a blessed mother. God is not dead. God is watching you. Don't you think that's why your Aki is safe? I pray for the best for you."

The judge took us home, back to Bibi's place.

When he left, I was happy to have Aki back, but didn't understand the implications and complications of this situation. It was a big puzzle—I didn't really understand what was going on. If the judge was so kind, why didn't he take all of us to live with him? Why didn't Aki stay there? If she didn't want to stay, what was wrong with her coming back home? I wished that Parviz would come and save us, like a knight in *Shah-zadeh-asb-savar* (shining armor), but Parviz was a fake man, not a savior.

It was afternoon and I was lying on the bed. I heard Bibi's husky voice talking to Mom behind the door, and then they came into the room. I turned my face to the wall, and pretended to be in a deep sleep. Even Mom believed I was asleep and covered me with a blanket.

Bibi ordered Mom to sit down saying, "Don't make anything for me because I don't have much time."

Mom wanted to make special tea, and although there was little time I knew Mom would make the tea anyway; she had her own rules for honoring a guest.

While she was making the tea, in her absence, Bibi said, "I wish they were dead." I think she was pointing at my back.

Then she said, "While her father was alive, all the money was for her. And now she wants money for her children also."

My heart started to beat hard and I was very angry, but I had to pretend to stay asleep.

Mom came in with the tea and said, "I make this special tea for you like I made it for my father, because he loved it."

Bibi asked, "Do you remember Dr. Vaziri, the pharmacist?"

My mom said, "Of course, he's one of your cousins."

Bibi reminded her, "Remember how much he loved you,

and your father didn't let you marry him because he was a known Communist?"

Mom remembered, "Oh, yes, my father was very strict about that. But my poor father didn't know how bad his son-in-law was; at least Dr. Vaziri didn't deny his involvement. But my children's father always showed two faces. He was a charlatan."

Then Bibi pointed to me and said, "These kids are his genes, and you're killing yourself for them."

Mom said, "No, they are my genes also; they are just innocent children. They are different than their father."

Bibi continued, "Anyhow, you know Dr. Vaziri never married, and he sent me here to ask you to marry him. He is a rich man, he is a very good investor, and if you marry him he can manage and increase our money."

Mom said, "What about my children?"

Bibi said, "Children? Look, Aki's breasts are the size of apples. (Unconsciously I touched mine and thought they were like small lemons). They are not kids anymore. I want you to leave them with their father and marry Vaziri. When you get control of the house maybe you can bring them. Who knows?"

Mom said, "No way. I want my children with me and I want them safe. I think my father left enough money for me to raise them without asking anybody else to feed them."

Bibi continued bitterly, "You are a very stubborn woman. I wish you were dead like your father because you are ruining our name. You shouldn't put your dad's last name on these kids. That money should be for my three sons and my daughter. I have to raise them and pay for their higher education. You're wasting that money on your children."

Mom said, "Did I ever ask for your children's share? Why are you so mean? I only want my own share, and haven't asked for more."

Bibi said, "I'm ashamed to tell everyone in the family that you became a servant. You humiliate your brothers and your sister by choosing this position, because you're selfish and want to be with your children no matter what! You think you are a hero? They are not proud of you. When I come to this house I try not to be seen."

Mom burst into tears, "You're acting like I'm a prostitute."

Bibi said, "I wish you were capable enough to be a prostitute. At least you would be making more money!"

And Mom called out, "Oh, God, be my witness to what she says!"

I couldn't stand it anymore. I cried out loudly, and Mom jumped up, came over and held me. I pretended that I'd had a bad dream. She wiped my eyes and said, "Oh, daydreams are never true. What was your dream?"

I told her that in my dream a big truck hit Bibi and crushed her face. I don't know how I made that up, but it explained my feelings.

Mom didn't calm me down, but instead calmed down Bibi by saying, "This dream means you are going to live longer."

She always took the side of the person I was fighting with, and it felt like she was against me at this moment. I was mad at Mom and Bibi, and I left the room. I took refuge at the willow tree. It was like a holy place for me when I was anxious, to confess everything and reflect. I felt a lot of rejection. Everyone who wanted Mom didn't want us—Shazdeh, our father, Vaziri. In every situation I saw that we children were a burden on my mother's ability to live her life.

I wondered to the willow tree, "My father doesn't want us. Vaziri doesn't want us. Shazdeh doesn't want us. Why did we come into this world to make life miserable for Mom? I didn't ask for this life. Who gave this awful life to me and my sisters? We children are the victims of this situation."

As I spoke to the willow tree, I remembered that my mom had a protector in her father that I didn't have. This reminded me of the sour cherry story.

Mom said her father had a garden of sour cherry trees, and the rule was that nobody touched the tree until the workers picked the cherries and boxed them for sale. Then, whatever was left was used for the household.

Mom remembered that her grandmother used to pick some of the cherries early, before the harvest, to make a special sour cherry jam as a favorite treat. She thought Bibi knew, but didn't care.

One day in a family gathering, Bibi started to mention that she thought some of the sour cherries were picked without respecting the rule. She tried to make a big deal of it, saying, "I want to know who's picking those cherries early. The sour cherries don't matter, but the rule matters."

Everyone looked at one another, and Bibi imitated a smart judge. "OK, we will look at everyone's hands, so we can see the blue stain of sour cherries."

She asked everyone to show their hands. This put mom's Grandmother in a very difficult situation, because she was a respected old woman who never expected to be attacked in such a harsh way.

Bibi said, "Oh, you see the blue mark of the sour cherry?"

And Mom's grandmother groaned, "I just made jam for Hajar, my granddaughter."

My grandfather's face became beet red and Mom could see all his veins standing out.

My grandfather said, "You know what? Those sour cherry trees all belong to my dead wife Setareh, and after her death they all now belong to her mother. She was the one who let us pick and sell the cherries. So Bibi has no right to put us through this interrogation."

When Mom was fired, Shazdeh's house sank into chaos. Nothing was in the right place, and nothing got done. Banoo, Shazdeh's daughter, was married and gone. Parviz was drafted and had left. The rest of the servants had no direction or organization. The household was crying for Mom's management. Shazdeh sent person after person to bring Mom back; she could keep both her daughters, after all.

Mom and I returned to the Qajar's house. The judge had already brought Aki back. The new environment was changed because neighbors started to gossip, and even Shazdeh's family treated Aki as though she were no longer a virgin. Shazdeh's attitude changed when he found out that Aki was now a divorcee. He started to pursue her—even though he was a 65 year old narcissist.

When Mom came to our room late one day, Aki reported, "Mom, it's funny because Shazdeh was sitting in the yard while I was playing, and he came over and held my hand. He said how beautiful I was, and that he loved me, and he wants to have me forever. He said the judge was a bad man because he divorced me, but if I were to marry him, I won't have to go away. Then he tried to get close and touch and kiss me, but I escaped and hid somewhere. When he left the garden, I ran to tell you."

Mom worried aloud, "Now what? How can I take care of these girls? This 65 year old man—shame on him!"

As it turned out, Parviz' father, at 65 years old, had chosen Aki for himself, and for a long time made overtures to her, and tried to win her over, telling her he would protect her family. She was very smart and protected herself by rejecting him each time he approached.

At the beginning of the fall, Aki and I went to register for school. To register we had to show our birth certificates, and Aki's now showed that she was a divorcée. They wouldn't register her.

The headmistress told Mom, "She is not a girl anymore, but a woman. She's been married. And now you want me to put her in a class with innocent girls? No."

For Aki, who loved school, reading, and math; this was total rejection, and nearly ruined her life. She would have gone to middle school, so I already had the expectation of her not being with me. But for her, staying home while everyone was going to school, especially Beeta from across the street talking about school and friends, changed Aki a lot. She became depressed and isolated, and impatient with me. She lost all interest in reading and became very lazy, staying in bed late, and arguing with Mom all the time. Mom had her own problems dealing with the situation, and sometimes I thought Ashi was the lucky one, not being with us. There was no more help with homework, and no fun.

After several months, a local tailor needed some help, so Mom offered Aki. Aki hated it, even though she had talent. It was too hard because this replaced the school that she loved. The tailor didn't tolerate her because she was miserable. Aki decided to make herself busy by hairdressing, which took her away from the house and Shazdeh's advances. Aki's desires were always very high, but destiny struggled with her.

Mom was very disappointed that Parviz did not have the courage to act on his love for Aki, and she gave up on him. Aki was disturbed about Shazdeh bothering her all the time. Many of the lower-class, uneducated neighborhood men proposed to her. Aki found it humiliating to have no proper educated suitors. She finally buried her soul deep inside and decided to marry, so she could be relieved of Shazdeh's advances and Mom and I could survive until I finished my education. At the age of 15, Aki decided to marry the first person who asked. He was a young local barber, 22 years old, named Akbar. He was athletic and handsome, sweet and outgoing. Right away he captured Mom's heart. Aki sacrificed for our family. Later she told me that she knew that she was not going to be happy or satisfied, but it was like the draft, with no choice for her.

I was sitting and playing on the steps, thinking about Aki now married, and Mom was making tomato sauce. It was in the middle of summer. There was a huge pot with a fire underneath, and a big spoon like a shovel for stirring. 100 boxes of tomatoes. It took the whole day to boil the sauce down to a thick paste that would be stored in two or three large glass jars in the cool basement, and used the whole year. Mom washed the tomatoes, put them in the pot, salted them, and then boiled them. She praised me when I helped to crush the tomatoes or pluck out the blossoms. Mom was sitting and stirring when Parviz, now in the last month of his draft in Northern Iran (an area of Rasht), came home for vacation.

He greeted Mom, pretending to help stir so he could have a private talk.

"How could you do that to me?"

Mom said, "What?"

Parviz asked, "Couldn't you wait for me to finish the draft? Why did you let Aki marry?"

Mom started to sob. "Why is everybody blaming me? Don't you know that your father fired me, and we had no place to go? He found your letter, and that was the end of my job here."

He became more polite, and asked, "What did my father say?"

"Your father forced me to get rid of Aki, saying there was not enough room for three of us. He said I would have to give one away. He left me with no choice, except to go back to my stepmother."

She then yelled at him, "You know, I raised you like my son. I had a son named Parviz who died at five years old. And one reason I agreed to become a servant and work here was because of you, and because your mom died. You were exactly his age. Couldn't you do something, and who do you think I would love to be my son-in-law more than you?"

He said, "How should I know these things? I didn't know what to do."

"You're an educated man, you're an engineer. Didn't you know what to do?"

"I didn't have the courage. People have always done things for me."

"So, why didn't you ask your father?"

He groaned, "You know my family. They would never let me marry Aki. And my father said that Aki had an arranged marriage with someone else, and I should stay away."

Mom said, "Please leave us alone and don't let Aki know your feelings. She is three months pregnant. You must let her live her own life now. And I promise to leave this house before you marry someone other than Aki. I will not stay here and watch you be married to someone else."

Parviz looked very sad and disappointed—his face got red like the tomatoes. He took that large spoon (like a shovel) from Mom's hands, looked at her and said, "Please sit for a moment, I'm going to help you with this."

That was the first man that I saw offer help to my mom, and I was touched by this gesture.

Malak-Banoo and her husband were remodeling their house, preparing for their new baby. They were in a rush to have it ready before their child was born. The changes in the house added new windows and bright, cheerful colors. She used to take me out with her to buy baby clothing, linens and curtains to decorate. She had excellent taste, and selected delicate and rich textures like velvet and satin, and colors of deep pink, fuchsia and purple. She was extremely happy, anticipating her baby's birth. I substituted Malak-Banoo for Aki in my life. Malak-Banoo made time for me, and we were busy together, enjoying her glorious life. I was part of it, but also compared it to Aki's.

Aki was also waiting for a baby. Aki shared a small, three bedroom house with her brother-in-law and his wife, and her mother-in-law. The house was located in a very busy shopping area (bazaar), a very old town in the middle of Shemiron. The neighborhood was called *Dezasheeb*, with two-story homes and small, dry yards. Aki's house had two persimmon trees, one on each side of the door. They had a small vegetable garden between the two trees, and on the side of the house was a small area to wash clothes, hands, everything.

Aki made a secure, portable sleeper for carrying the baby, with a very nice baby blanket. She hand-made baby clothes and decorated them with lace. She put these items in a trunk in the corner of the room, in preparation for the baby's arrival.

My role was to watch these two extremely opposite situations. Two women I loved, two babies arriving, one to a whole house and the other to a basket in the corner. What a contrast.

With the change of seasons, I lost all my friends—trees, flowers and frogs. Everyone left me and I felt lonely. Malak-Banoo and Davood-Khan were looking for a nursemaid. I remember one afternoon Malak-Banoo, her father, and my mom were talking about who to hire. Malak-Banoo asked Mom to stay with her for a few days when she came home from the hospital.

I jumped into the conversation, "What about me? I'm not going to stay here alone!"

Malak-Banoo's father (Shazdeh) said, "You're a big girl now and you can take care of the house while your mom is taking care of Malak-Banoo. I looked at him and I wished him dead. I whispered to myself, "I'm not going to stay here with you, narcissist."

One evening after the first snow, I heard everyone rushing and running around. Malak-Banoo had pain. It was time to deliver the baby. Mom rushed to take the Qur'an and holy water, and did her own private ritual of rubbing the tummy, giving a sip of water and passing the Qur'an over Malak-Banoo's head. Davood-Khan, Malak-Banoo's husband, and her brother, Parviz, warmed the car. Shazdeh was trying to calm her down. She was moaning, and Mom carried the suitcase.

I was asking, "Can I come with you? Mom, are you going with her?"

Mom angrily responded, "Of course! Who do you THINK is going to go with her?" (She didn't have any mother or sister.)

So I said, "Yes, you will be her mother and I will be her sister."

As usual, Mommy told me not to argue but go to sleep, because there was school the next day. She left me alone, wondering and scared.

Mom sat on one side of Malak-Banoo holding her hand and praying. Shazdeh was on the other side, helping her get into the car. I didn't give up trying, and finally Parviz told me to get my coat and come along. I just flew to my room, grabbed my coat, and pushed myself into the back seat.

The hospital was called *Najmieh*. In the car, Parviz and Davood-Khan were saying that Malak-Banoo's doctor was Dr. Mossadeq's son and that the hospital belonged to Dr. Mossadeq's mother, one of the Qajar's family. They talked about how precious Dr. Mossadeq was to the country; he was now in prison because of the coup. (He spent three years in a solitary cell, and the rest of his life in house arrest in *Ah-Mad-Abad*.) They discussed how fortunate the country would be if Dr. Mossadeq were allowed to continue to rule the government in his proud way.

In the back seat, Malak-Banoo's face was turning from red to normal to red to normal. She was squeezing Mom's hand on one side, and Shazdeh's hand on the other. It was like watching a movie. I observed everything. I remember everything they were talking about, very cool conversation in the front seat, and lots of painful looks in the back seat. Each time that she had a contraction her face became very red, warm and sweaty, and it was scary for me. I thought each time, "That's it—we're going to lose her."

On the other hand, the back seat action couldn't take my

attention away from the conversation about Dr. Mossadeq. I just pictured him in my mind like my mother's father, and I could picture them together under the willow tree. Even though I was a child, I had a lot of feeling for Mossadeq.

Finally we got to the hospital which was modern, clean and bright, with newly educated doctors and nurses and private rooms available. They brought a stretcher and took Malak-Banoo in. Five of us were sitting in the hallway, and Malak-Banoo just looked at us with pain and wanted Mom to go with her. But they wouldn't let Mom go; they were mentioning a new word, possible Caesarian section.

We were there about two or three hours. Mom occupied herself reading the Qur'an and praying. Davood, the expectant father, was pacing through the hallway, and I started asking Parviz a lot of questions about Dr. Mossadeq. He was surprised that I was so interested. I told him I learned from Dr. Dashti and Beeta's father, and everybody was saying wonderful things about him; I didn't know him but I liked him very much. Finally, one of the most beautiful pictures in my life came when they brought out the baby. They called us to the infant room from behind the window where we could see the baby boy. I connected with two black, big eyes and from that moment, Majid held a special place in my heart.

Until Majid was born, I couldn't imagine what was in Aki's tummy. But now I went to visit her every day, and it was like I could see the baby right through her skin. I loved that baby before it was born.

When it was time for Aki's delivery, I was in Aki's house, and unfortunately Mom was involved with her job, and not able to help Aki at this special moment.

It was very cold, there was lots of snow and school was closed. All the trees were frost-covered and icicles were hanging from the branches and gutters. The only people with Aki were me, her mother-in-law, two of her sisters-in-law and the experienced, unlicensed country mid-wife.

They prepared the room for delivery. They covered a corner with sheep skin, and placed two bricks on it. A basin, towel, soap and water were nearby. The midwife brought Aki in to sit on the sheep skin, and asked me to leave.

They said, "You're too young to witness this."

Outside, there was a small stone fire pit in the back yard to heat water and cook food when there was company. Above the wood fire, was a huge pot of boiling water. The snow made it difficult for the helpers to go in and out.

I was eating the snow, warming my hands over the water and enjoying crunching the *ghandeel* (icicles) like candy, feeling very warm enjoying the steam of the water on my face.

Suddenly I remembered that Aki was having a baby and got worried about what was happening inside. I sneaked in and hid in an adjoining, curtained storage room where Aki had her extra mattresses. I pushed a small opening between two curtain panels to watch.

Malak-Banoo's delivery started playing like a movie in my mind. I remembered Mom praying behind the door for her. Now Aki was in this small room without Mom and with these unprofessional people. It was such a primitive setting. Through a hole in the curtain I watched, feeling that I was with my sister and praying for her all the time.

"Oh, my God, how will she have a baby in this room

without any medical personnel or equipment?" I wanted to make the opening in the curtain wider and wider so I could see everything but was afraid they would put me out if I made a sound or move. I was scared for myself and for Aki. With wide open eyes I witnessed "where the baby comes from."

They put sheep skins under Aki and they put one brick on each side of the skin. The midwife pushed Aki to squat on top of the bricks on each side of the sheepskin. On one side was one sister-in-law and on the other side was the other sister-in-law. In the back, her mother-in-law was stroking her back, praying and telling her when to push. The mid-wife was trying to deliver the baby. Aki was in enormous pain. Her face was contorted and changing color. She was sweating a lot, but completely silent. God knows how many times I wanted to jump from that storage closet and hold her hand. It was so difficult for me to watch and not touch her. The in-laws were so helpful, but I think if they weren't there I would have torn that curtain and reached for Aki. As soon as I saw the baby's head I couldn't stay there anymore and I jumped into the room. They all started yelling and swearing at me, but they didn't have time to be involved with me. I reached for Aki and held her head. I kissed her forehead and wished Mom was there to read the Qur'an and give her that holy water. After Aki delivered the baby, she just fainted.

The baby was blond with small, golden eyes just like his mother.

The contrast was so interesting. Even though Malak-Banoo didn't have a mother, she had my mother with her. And although Aki had a mother, she didn't have her mom at the time she needed her because she was busy providing for Malak-Banoo.

They brought warm water from outside, washed the baby in a basin, and then washed Aki. They gave the baby to her, and then she gave Ali to me to hold. He is named Ali after my mother's father, Haj-Ali.

Mom came to visit Aki after her delivery. She made *kachi* for her and brought her a beautiful green dress as a gift for Aki to keep forever. She kissed Aki and then looked at Ali's face.

She said, "Oh, my sweet ruby. I love you."

When Prince Shazdeh passed away I was almost 16. Now the mansion belonged to the 28 year old brothers. They were identical twins, tall with light brown hair combed straight back. They looked elegant with their dark brown eyes and thin Roman nose. Parviz was born first, and was well-mannered and down to earth. Bahram, the second-born, was very arrogant and self-centered. After their father's death they quickly transitioned from boys to young men blossoming into adulthood. They changed their way of life in search of the key to happiness.

Their sister, Malak-Banoo, had died of liver cancer three years after her son Majid's birth. She had always accepted me like the sister she never had. She mentored me and taught me about a modern way of life. But now she left me alone in the world. She was my princess and role model; I grieved deeply. I gravitated to Majid in an effort to keep her alive for myself.

Even after their sister's tragic death, her brothers' grief didn't stop them from expressing their new gregarious and modern lifestyle. They found out that life is more about pleasure and fun. It seemed as though they had been slaves of the old Qajar culture, and now they were free of family pressure to maintain the old traditions.

It was the '60s, full of fun, music, dancing, and hippies. There was a lot of influence from the West—music, film, magazines and clothing styles, even in our village north of Tehran. With the two brothers' encouragement, I started to bring my teenage friends to the house and arranged parties for all of us. The two brothers enjoyed meeting my friends and this now became the real home that I had always wished for. My dream of being a princess was realized.

The brothers bought a record player for the house. They were more than happy to buy the most popular records and play them for our parties. They decorated one big room with the disco lights that changed colors, and emptied it of furniture so it was always ready for dancing. I couldn't believe these two boring men had changed so much when they were around me—into two lively teenagers. Perhaps they were compensating for the teenage years they had missed when their father was alive.

I loved dancing rock and roll. I loved the Beatles. I also had a large poster of Marilyn Monroe in my small room at the end of the garden. We all were young and happy, and this beautiful house was every teenager's dream. For this reason I was the most popular kid in high school. Girls were dying to be invited by me to bring their male friends to these parties. Mom was supportive of these gatherings because she loved fun as much as we did, and now she could supervise me from the background. She made the best cold sandwiches for us. Alcohol was prohibited, although I knew some of the guests brought their own drinks and drank privately.

One winter day we had one of our parties. Parviz and I went to pick up a friend who lived close to Aki. On the way, Parviz suggested stopping the car by her house so we could just see her for a moment. He wanted to go in, so I went to check if it was OK. When I went in, Aki was lying under the *corsi* (table with the cover) and was very pale. She said she thought she was pregnant so she went to a country midwife and had been given some pills that caused her to bleed a lot. She was very scared and called the doctor who had arrived just before I did. He gave her a shot to stop the bleeding and advised her to drink lots of water and rest as much as possible. I told Aki that I was with Parviz and he wanted to come in and see her.

She hid her face under the blanket and said, "Oh, no, not when I am in this condition—no, no."

I also didn't wish Parviz to see Aki so broken and weak. I hurriedly excused myself and left Aki alone.

I sat in the car and told Parviz she was busy and we could not see her. As he started the car, he sighed loudly and seemed very disappointed. I felt like a selfish jerk, and thought I should have found a way to get Parviz and Aki to see one another. But she wasn't ready. I felt deep in my heart their hidden love for each other, but didn't do anything to help. Was I trying to protect my sister from getting hurt again? Or was I maintaining our family pride and strength by not allowing Parviz to see Aki in a miserable situation? I hated myself for leaving my sister alone and not even mentioning it to Mom, because I was the host and didn't want to ruin the party.

We went home to the loud music and girls and boys dancing rock and roll (*Hit the Road, Jack*). I took Parviz's hands.

"Oh, this is my favorite music!" I pretended there was nothing wrong.

Parviz said, "Oh no, I am so old for this kind dance."

He grabbed my friend's brother who was sitting quietly, put my hand in his, and told him,

"Here is my sister—a very good dancer."

My heart melted. This was the first time in my life that I felt my dead brother Parviz was alive because he called me his sister.

That night I was full of guilt for neglecting and leaving my beloved sister alone and in pain—emotional and physical. My over-sensitive antenna was focused on Parviz all night. He looked very preoccupied and sad; I saw him drinking in the hallway. Outside was covered with heaps of snow while guests inside were enjoying great fun. I appeared to be very happy, but it was a mask that hid my guilt and sadness. I tried to do my best to manage difficult situations to maintain balance, and it became my pattern to appear as if nothing bad was happening—always trying to keep the hurt away.

One of the things I enjoyed each summer was seeing Majid, Malak-Banoo's son. When he was born I was 13 years old, and I watched him from the days when his mom was breast feeding him. I remember his big eyes were focused on his mom's eyes and he would grab her finger and suck milk vigorously. God knows how much I loved him. Now he was a cute and lively four year old with thick black hair and light skin, and a beautiful dimpled smile. He had very ruddy cheeks like apples and he was always happy to see me. He would jump up and down and welcome me in a way that made me want to see him often.

His father, Davood-Khan, liked me to spend time with them

and trusted me to be a good influence and keep Majid safe. On weekends he gave me money to take Majid out and have ice cream, buy toys or go to the photo shop and take pictures. I helped Majid learn reading, writing and other things. At four, Majid had two home teachers—one for music and one for reading and writing—and sometimes he needed my help.

Every weekend that we didn't have a party I spent with Majid. I was able to play like a four year old when I was with him. He didn't have any other playmates. Sometimes during the week I took him to Aki's house to play with her son, Ali. Majid had a lot of fine toys brought from Europe. We put some of the toys in a bag and took them to play with Ali. It was a special time for Ali who had few toys, and he always waited for us to come. We made a very nice triangular friendship: Ali, Majid and me. Aki, who also had a one year old daughter, appreciated my help on those days. When we were there she cooked us the best food and made us feel like special guests.

One day when Majid's teacher was there and they were working silently, I saw a girl my age sneak out through the back door.

The housekeeper told me, "I feel so bad for Majid. His father, Davood, brings these dirty girls to the house every night and I told him he shouldn't do this. He should get a life and marry you. You love Majid and would be a wonderful wife."

When she talked this way she ruined my relationship with Majid. I was only 17 years old. What was she talking about? I loved this baby but couldn't be his mother—he was like my little brother.

I gave her a very bad look and told her, "If I come over here, it is only for Majid. Why is your brain painting this scenario?

It's crazy!" I picked up my coat and purse and wanted to leave. I couldn't stay there any more.

Majid's father came to me and said, "Don't leave. I'll give you a ride."

I said, "No, I want to go home."

Davood-Khan said, "Why are you so red and angry? What happened?"

Before I answered, the housekeeper said, "She's not angry. She's excited because I told her what you told me. She would be the best mother for Majid."

He laughed and said, "Yes, this is my idea. Why didn't you let me tell her?"

Then I said, "I just want to leave. I don't want to stay here any more."

I went to Majid to kiss him. He was so busy with his teacher he didn't notice. I rushed out of the house and went home by bus. I cried all the way—humiliated and disillusioned.

My world with Majid was ruined. I left part of me there. If I wanted to see Majid again, I would have to step into the filth of his father. I thought of the judge bringing Aki back to Mom, saying it wasn't *hallal* because she was so young and innocent. I was thinking the same thing for myself. I wasn't *hallal* for Davood-Khan. When I got home I hid under a blanket so Mom would not see my red eyes and ask me what happened. I dreamed I was in my garden.

It was still summertime on a weekend and we were sitting in the garden near the kitchen. Mom used to buy raisins in a burlap gunny sack, rinse them in a colander with the hose, then lie them out on a clean sheet to pull the stems off. Then she put them in another sheet to dry again in the sun. She did this job so delicately that it took all my attention to watch her, but I wasn't allowed to touch any unless I was given a plate. It was a very simple thing, but I loved it and it was relaxing—nothing important and yet very fundamental to everyday life.

The doorbell rang and I opened the door. It was Majid and his father, Davood-Khan. Majid hugged me tightly and wouldn't let me go—he was so happy to see me and I was thrilled to see him.

Davood-Khan said he wanted to speak with Mom. As soon as the twin brothers knew it was Davood-Khan, they came out and they all sat around a table under the willow tree. Mom asked me to bring tea for them, and then I took Majid and sat by Mom to help her. Mom offered raisins to Majid and he was so happy. He put many raisins in his mouth at once and we laughed.

They called Mom to their table to sit by them. My heart started beating and I knew this was about Davood-Khan's proposal. Majid used to play with my watch, so to be able to hear the other conversation, I gave him the watch. I was not far from them and could read their expressions and gestures. Sitting face to face with Bahram, Davood-Khan was sitting proudly with his legs crossed, shaking his foot. He had a pipe in his mouth and sometimes he pointed to me or my mom. Parviz looked very focused and surprised. Bahram looked like he was negotiating to sell a slave like the master of the house. Sometimes he was so excited that his face changed color and he gazed sneakily toward me. Mom seemed very nervous, playing with her buttons and looking around at me and the sky. The atmosphere seemed very tense.

I went to make sure Majid was OK, and then went back to where I could observe. He was ruining my watch, taking it apart. I thought it was OK since my life was being ruined as well. I told Majid that he had to fix my watch and then give it back unless he sat still and waited for me.

Then I went out to the table and pointed at Davood-Khan. "I know why this man is here. He already told me what he wants and I clearly rejected him. Don't you understand that "No" means "No"?!" My eyes filled with tears as I told Mom that he was very manipulative.

Again I pointed to Davood-Khan and said, "You think you can have whatever you want! The whole world doesn't belong to you."

Mom stood up and hushed me, shooing me away.

Then I turned to my mom. "You are so selfish. I am 16 now and you are talking about my future without getting me involved." She was shocked, looking at me with wide open eyes, just like she saw me for the first time.

Now I pointed to Bahram. "Hey you! You are egotistical, narcissistic, and self-absorbed. All you do is please yourself like a prince, resting on your family's heritage."

He stood up with closed fists. "Stop right there or I will beat you up like nobody has done before."

Parviz rushed toward him and held him tightly, calling my name and saying, "Shh... shh... Calm down."

I was fuming and burning. Aki and Ashi's life were playing in my mind like a movie. Mom came towards me holding my hand and saying, "Stop...stop. What is wrong with you today? Why are you acting so crazy?"

I ignored her. I remembered Malak-Banoo's 6 years of tragic living with this man and yelled at him.

"You are a jerk! You pretend that you are a gentleman but you are a bastard. You always betrayed your wife; you had a mistress when she was alive and you even brought a hooker home when she was sick, you graceless devil!"

He became flushed and looked around to see if other servants were watching.

I continued, summoning the bravery from my Grandfather under the willow tree, "Even your housekeeper knew how much Malak-Banoo suffered. Go ask your neighbors! They all knew what an unfaithful rat you were! She always was worried about her only son Majid. Now you jackass and bastard, are after me! And talking about my mother's salvation! You'd better take care of your own low life and pray for your own salvation. I hope God keeps Majid's life safe from you!"

Everybody looked shocked with surprised, stunned and motionless faces. I could feel very heavy tension surrounding us. I felt exhausted and tears were pouring down my cheeks as if I was suffocating. I broke down and sobbed while I escaped out of the garden towards the nearby strawberry farm. When I reached the farm, I dropped down on a big, flat stone on which Mom used to sit and feed the homeless dogs. She always brought leftover food for them. I was breathless and worn out but very satisfied. Two puppies came up and started to lick my hands and feet. Such a warm feeling. I felt extremely released and free but not at all sure what was going to happen to me and Mom the next day.

After that proposal things were never the same. Parviz and Bahram stopped seeing their brother-in-law and of course I was forbidden to see Majid anymore. Bahram was very aloof and ignored me whenever he saw me. Losing Majid was intolerable for me and the world seemed cruel and unfair.

I was nervous about what would happen to me when I finished high school. I couldn't see any future for myself in the picture. Some people around me were thinking about arranging a marriage. I hated that and rejected each introduction in ways that hurt others' feelings.

I started to look for a job before finishing high school. I saw an ad in the newspaper for a drug company representative and took it to Dr. Dashti. The company was looking for high school students. As usual, Dr. Dashti had a very open heart and told me I needed some education for this job. He offered to teach me about the job if I came to his office when I could after school. I started to learn about the drugs and their names and formulas. He also sent me out to the front office with other visitors to learn presentation skills. I studied the whole summer of 11th grade. Dr. Dashti tested me himself and I passed his tests. Then I filled out the application for that company with Dr. Dashti's written support. Through that company I met a lot of doctors and also some powerful people. I was so grateful. During this time I began to find my real self and to know who I was and what I wanted in my life.

I was trained and worked in Pahlavi General Hospital, the largest hospital in Tehran. People used to call it "the hospital with 1000 beds." It was located in the center of Tehran, on 58.2 acres of land, and it opened in 1946. Outstanding physicians and professors were hired by the government, and scientific and economic experts soon flocked to the center to make it similar to other international hospitals around the world.

The nursing school had a dormitory for girls and I roomed with two stunning and talented girls named Mehry and Gretel. We had a beautiful school with a pool and many other amenities. It was located beside Pahlavi General Hospital (now called Khomeini General Hospital). We shared classes with the hospital staff, who came to teach in our classrooms. We had practicum in the hospital. Our time was evenly divided between studying and practice. There was no summer vacation, so we could complete our academic work in three years, because the country needed nurses desperately. The hospital was growing fast and there were few institutions which were training nurses. Our curriculum was intertwined with Tehran University's course offerings. It was very hard and intense, but also lots of fun because we were all young, and we spent day and night together. I was a very good student and studied hard.

On May 1, 1968, I started to work in the operating room. I'd always wanted to work as a scrub nurse and witness an operation—except for an eye operation because the eye is so delicate that I was very uncomfortable with anyone touching it. However, my first assignment was in the eye operation room and I had no choice but to accept it. I was a 22 year old, well trained nurse with confidence in myself.

During my training I had seen many kinds of operations but not an eye surgery. One morning I was assigned to assist the scrub nurse. We set the operating table with surgical tools, and then the scrubbed surgeon came in with the other interns and med students to start the operation. One intern started to clean up around the injured eye then the surgeon asked for the bistoury, a narrow sharp surgical knife to cut the tissue. As soon as the scrub nurse handed the knife to the surgeon, I felt lightheaded and dizzy, and then fainted.

One of the interns patted my face asking if I was OK. When I opened my eyes I saw two of the most kind, concerned eyes looking back at me.

He asked me, "Did you have breakfast this morning?"

I said, "Yes."

"Is this your first time in the OR?"

"This is the first time I am in the eye unit."

"OK, so this happens! Soon you will get used to it."

The chief doctor joked to change the mood, "You chose the right one to faint onto! Believe me, this was the best choice."

We all laughed and I was embarrassed. The chief told one

of the nurses to take me to the recovery room to relax for a while before returning to work.

I thought, "I wanted to show my professionalism and what a wonderful nurse I was. What a disturbing moment on my first day at a new job."

While I was lying on the recovery bed I thought of that intern's eyes that looked very familiar. It seemed I had known him for a long time. I was curious where I had seen him before. His eyes flashed repeatedly in my mind and I became preoccupied thinking where I must have met him. One hour later he came to check on me. He felt my pulse and then touched my forehead to see if I had a fever. Then he took his stethoscope and leaned over to hear my heart. My eyes were closed and I felt butterflies in my stomach.

He said, "No problem. You can go back to work now."

I opened my eyes. He had a perfect smile on his face. I thanked him and his eyes seemed very focused on me. This moment became tattooed in my mind.

I went to the bathroom, combed my hair and washed my face—remembering those eyes in the pool of water gathered in my hands.

The day after, Dr. Behrooz found me and asked how I was doing. I smiled and answered that I was fine.

He asked, "Have we worked together before? You look so familiar to me."

I said, "No, but I had the same feeling." I was very shy.

That May was unexpectedly rainy and the rain washed the operating room windows, surprising everyone including me. We worked together every day and he showed me more and more attention by asking questions and teaching me things that I didn't know or subjects that I was curious about. I could feel a growing friendship between us. Some of the doctors and nurses joked around in order to deal with the daily stress, the heavy work schedules and huge responsibilities. He was one of them, but he showed me a more poetic and romantic side of himself. I enjoyed his different attention and responded with growing affection.

The following month I was assigned to the night shift, which matched his schedule—perhaps hidden hands were arranging this coincidence? One night early in June, when I arrived at my office, the familiar smell of jasmine wafted through the room. My desk was covered with little, delicate pinkish-white flowers. I was accustomed to the smell of ether in that room, but tonight was all heavenly jasmine, my favorite and most loved flower. I wondered if this was for me. Who knew me so well? The night shift was so boring so this surprise was a blessing. I wondered who else could love jasmine the way I did. I started reading the update report when Dr. Behrooz, my intern friend, arrived.

He looked at me and said, "Do you like the smell?"

I said, "Yes but I don't know who put so much jasmine on my desk!"

He said, "Maybe someone who thinks you're very delicate and smell like jasmine."

I was too shy to say anything more.

In Tehran, most girls have very beautiful tan skin, but girls from the north of Iran, especially Ardebil, are popular for their pinkish-white and soft skin. Dr. Behrooz distinguished me in this way and through his words and action told me my delicate coloring was special to him.

That month, I frequently found a different type of flower

on my desk, reading my mind and feelings. Considering my deep, internal relationship with flowers, even imagining them as relatives, nothing could have touched my feelings more than this. Little by little, I was falling in love with him.

I took care of the flowers very well. Some flowers had stems and could go in a vase but jasmine floated in a bowl. In the morning I would wrap the petals in a towel and put them in the refrigerator. The next night I would take them out to enjoy my relationship with them again.

Behrooz did uncharacteristic things for a doctor. For example, he put the most passionate poetry on my desk for me but never said anything. I loved poetry and these poems softened the drudgery of hard work, like wearing ballet shoes to walk in the snow. I answered each poem with another poem—it was a lovely, quiet and mysterious relationship between us. I waited for him every night and if he wasn't there I felt empty and lonely, and hoped I'd have a very busy night so I would not feel this emptiness.

Turkish in Iran is like Spanish in the United States. There are many Turkish dialects and accents such as Kurdish, Azari and Shirazi that originated in a geographic location by which people identify their cultural group. In Tehran, where people from many different groups live, there is often a language barrier that results in Turks being treated like second-rate citizens, not because of their ability or intelligence, but because of the fear of misunderstanding. This results in isolation and discrimination.

One night, we had an emergency. The patient was an old Azari-Turk, a 52 year old man. He was diagnosed in the emergency room with acute appendicitis and sent to surgery. He couldn't speak Farsi and he was very frightened, praying all the time in Azari.

Behrooz went to him and spoke in Azari, "Don't be scared, *ghorkh-ma- Dada- jan* (dear father)."

I spoke Azari to him too and the patient calmed down and felt much better. His surgery was completed successfully.

That night Behrooz and I discovered our common Azari background, and we found out that both our fathers were involved with the Tudeh party of Iran. Between 1945-1946, during the Azerbaijani crisis, most of the members went underground to conduct their activities. Some of the members were captured or executed and some of them escaped from Iran to Russia. He was told that his father was killed while escaping. Many Azari families dissolved during that period—killed, divorced, separated—and the children left adrift. The country suffered the most.

Behrooz told this story about how his grandfather saved his daughter's (Behrooz's mother's) life.

"My father was a Communist. He was hidden in my grandfather's house. The government agent was after him. He tried to escape to Russia and was killed on his way. It was revealed that my mother was pregnant by this now-dead Communist. My grandfather escaped to Tehran with his sixteen year old pregnant daughter and the rest of his family." He sighed and continued, "My grandfather and his friend planned an arranged marriage for my widowed mother to marry his friend's son and I was adopted by him even before I was born."

To change the mood, he jokingly said, "Can you imagine what a lucky child I was, having two fathers even before I was born?"

I thought of my father, who was a Communist and who also escaped the country during that period. He survived and returned to Iran but left his family for another woman. He didn't divorce my mom and her wounded heart never recovered from this hurt.

So, I asked Behrooz, "Do you miss your father?"

He said, "Of course. I keep his picture in my room by my side."

"Even though you hadn't seen him?" I asked.

He said, "It doesn't matter, he was still my father." He really loved and respected his biological father as a fighter and hero.

We both agreed many Azari's lives were ruined during that crisis period. Then we were interrupted by another emergency situation. That night was a very busy night.

One day during an operation two of the doctors were talking about their gambling the night before and I joined their conversation.

I said, "I like poker." Behrooz looked at me over his glasses with a disapproving glance. I blushed and kept quiet. Later that day he apologized for his behavior and I told him I was annoyed. He said that he was surprised to see a lady like me join a conversation with those gamblers. It felt like he was taking an adult role and chastising me as a child, which made me even more confrontational. He asked if there were any more things he should know about me.

I was offended, rolled my eyes and said, "For your information: I am a good dancer. I pray only once at night instead of five times a day and I am a risky driver. Anything else you want to know? Why do you care anyway?"

He smiled and said, "Because you are a puzzle to me!"

He didn't know I was raised alongside the Qajar family and that I learned many things from them. Card games were a very enjoyable activity in some families. Every weekend the Qajar family gathered, set up six tables, and on each table guests played different games. This was a special opportunity for me to learn all the games by watching and later playing. Aki and I always watched curiously and later practiced together. We both were good players. Behrooz was not familiar with card playing at all. He said since tenth grade he prepared himself for medical school and was busy with the many required classes.

I said, "So you were a nerd?" Then he was paged.

In three months his schedule was changed and he asked me out.

He said, "When I was here I could see you but this is my last day in this unit and I want to see you outside of the hospital."

I accepted his offer gladly, because I wanted to see him too, and was waiting for this moment.

I grew up around women—no father, brothers or male relatives—except my mother's stepbrothers who I rarely saw. At the nursing boarding school we all were girls. So for me to escalate a close relationship with a man was very strange and difficult. I was scared of dating. But when he asked me out my heart filled with love, and although I was anxious, I embraced his offer. I went to my older sister Aki, who was married now, and told her the story. She was very happy for me and convinced me that I made the right decision to go out with him.

It was my first date ever and I was very nervous. I wanted to look my best to impress him. I tried on every dress I had and then chose a ruffled white shirt with a black mini skirt. I experimented with different styles for my hair and decided to leave it flowing down to my shoulders with a nice hair clip, very different from the operating room where we wore hats to hide our hair. Finally I left the apartment and took a taxi to Asia Hospital.

My mother and I lived in a small town in a one bedroom apartment, a home I proudly provided. It gave us a feeling of freedom. It was revolutionary for a young woman to be so independent, and able to support her mother and herself, even though it was difficult. I was admired by progressives but a source of curiosity for more traditional community members. Because we were living without a man, we were "supervised" by nosy neighbors, and they annoyed us. I explained the situation to Behrooz and we agreed that for each date he would pick me up in front of the Asia Hospital in the center of town where I worked a second job.

This was the first time I saw him wearing a suit instead of the white doctor's uniform. He looked very handsome. He came to me and held my hand for the first time. We went toward the car and he opened the door—a cultured and polite gentleman. He told me I looked gorgeous without my uniform. We went to Roudaki Hall to see Rashid Behbodof's concert of Russian classical music. The concert hall was elegant and beautiful. As the lights dimmed and the concert started, we got lost in the music, that loving music. Can he read my mind? This is the second touch—first the flowers, then the music—the two most important things in my life. I was listening with all my heart. The music washed away my anxiety.

Sometimes I watched him with his closed eyes listening to the music, and I was so impressed with his gentleness and maturity. He was not strange to me at all; it seemed I had known him all my life and I felt very comfortable beside him. His look, his intelligence, his passion, his politeness—he was just a perfect gift from God to me.

When the concert was finished he asked me to dinner. I refused by saying it was late and my mother would be worried.

He laughed and asked, "What about your father?" He didn't realize that my father had not been in my life since infancy.

To stop him asking more about my family's life, I made a deal with him.

I said, "Let us not ask about each other's families, because each time we talk about someone other than ourselves it means we must be bored and losing interest in each other!"

I knew that dating without knowing your date's background and family was not accepted in our culture, and that's why he seemed very surprised by my suggestion.

But he said, "It's an interesting point!"

He did not realize I was worried that if he found out about my family's past he would definitely be disappointed and disrespect and leave me. At 22 years old, my family was a liability whenever I met someone new even though I loved my family dearly. I just wanted to wash away the past and be the person I had become. I didn't cry for my past but I wished I could change it—and did so in my imagination—dragging everyone with me. In many ways, I am still challenged by this conflict within myself and keep pushing myself and others to change their view of themselves.

In the garden you prune plants and branches to make way for new growth and seasonal change. I didn't want to prune anything away from my life but I still wanted to change it.

We drove back home, passing the ruins of an ancient mosque.

We rarely talked about politics. He hated politics and his political ideas were opposite to mine. One time I asked him what he thought about the prior year's event of June 2, 1967, when a student was shot dead by a West Berlin policeman at a demonstration against the visiting Shah of Iran in Germany. This caused SAVAK (the Shah's secret police) to capture many activist students at Iran's universities.

He stopped me right there and warned, "Listen carefully. Please do not get involved with politics, because it is a very dirty business."

I interrupted him, "Are you a Savaki?"

He got angry and said, "No I am not a Savaki, nor an activist. When it comes to politics I become deaf and blind. Politicians are predators—that's just their nature. I believe I have to be careful and mind my own business. You will wound me if you talk more about politics and you better promise me never ever get involved."

I thought, "Wow! Such a strong reaction!"

He sounded very bitter and reminded me of my mother's

overreaction to anything political. Although I disagreed, I didn't argue. I thought, with three jobs in my hands, who would have time for politics anyway?

I used to talk about him to my sister a lot. In spite of the conflicts we had encountered thus far, I felt he was everything I could possibly want in a soul mate. I didn't want to lose Behrooz. Aki was very happy for me. She knew almost everything about him. She supported me in any way she could and gave me hope and motivation. We decided not to worry Mom with the information that I was dating someone.

Neither Behrooz nor I liked to speak on the phone, but we both enjoyed writing each other letters and continued seeing one another, even if only for a short time every day. By now I was working in three hospitals at once and I rarely had time for myself. He was very busy studying for his internist exam and working simultaneously. So our lives were matched. We were always short of time. We arranged for our break to be at the same time, and he gave me a ride from one hospital to another. We used this "car time" as a date and passed letters back and forth. The limited time actually made us feel more romantic toward one another. Although it was financially very difficult for me, I eventually decided to stop one job and continued with two. The salary at University Hospital was less than the private hospitals and I had a three year contract to get my license and be relieved of my loan obligation. That salary was only sufficient to pay the rent, so I kept my second job working in Asia Hospital, which was newly built, modern and privately owned by foreign-trained and specialized doctors. I liked working there. They paid a good salary and I had a higher position as a head nurse. I gained much more experience and knowledge at University Hospital, while Asia Hospital gave me a better quality of life. When I left the third hospital job, I had more time to spend with Behrooz and enjoy his company. He said my decision meant a lot to him and he appreciated our free time.

Every other day during our new free time, we hiked to Alborz Mountain, which was very close to my apartment and a twenty minute drive to work. We usually left at six in the morning and returned at eight to go to work. We also made a couple friends at the mountain and that made hiking more fun for us. He used to concentrate on every little thing along the way. Our friends teased him about how his eyes caught each delicate sight around us. He pointed at me and said that's why his eyes caught me.

On our way, while he was noticing every change in the scenery, I was always conscious of the surrounding aroma of leaves and wildflowers, and even the changes in the weather. I told them that when I was born, it was during the country's crisis. My mother didn't have any milk. Some offered to nurse me. My mother told me that I wouldn't accept milk from any woman who didn't smell like her. After that, my first olfactory memory was walking around huge vases of jasmine that inhabited the corners of the garden where I grew up. Jasmine became my blood sister, traveling through my feelings and moods. I have always loved jasmine.

Then Behrooz surprisingly said, "My stepfather's business is to sell raw materials for perfume and he brought home pure oils for us to smell. I fell in love with jasmine's fragrance as a child, too."

I thought of those jasmine flowers on my desk at work and knew that this was an unknown coincidence that had brought us closer to one another.

Another time we saw a scared, little bird with a broken wing that was not able to fly, hidden in the bushes. He picked it up and asked me to hold it, then ripped off a portion of his shirt. He made a bandage for the bird's wing and carried it down the mountain until he found a nest to hold the bird safely. This touched me so deeply that it brought tears to my eyes. We both were living in the womb of nature and lost ourselves together in this beautiful and natural world.

Hiking became one of our best hobbies. We continued our friendship with that couple. One time we went to see "The Graduate" at Empire State Cinema. The film had been dubbed into Farsi and had a very happy ending. I'll never forget Dustin Hoffman's romantic voice.

One evening we went out with them to the theater and to a restaurant. They told us their story. They met each other at work and they had been dating secretly for a year. Both of their families were very religious and fundamental and had prearranged plans for their futures. I thought those parents were seeking heaven for their children in hellish ways. This couple had plans to leave the country and get married in America if they had to. Behrooz was trying to tell them that they could convince their parents to understand that society had changed. The idea of prearrangement was old fashioned, and while it had some advantages, it had no meaning for couples who met and fell in love.

He said, "Sometimes prearranged marriage is the only solution, like when my father was killed, my grandfather and his friend found the best way to rescue my mother's life. They arranged a marriage for the 16 year old pregnant widow with an 18 year old young man who already was working for his father's company, was not going to continue his education and was ready to get married and have a family. Both parents were religious and thought this was a heavenly opportunity that God presented to them because a baby was involved. So they saved that baby too. That baby was me."

Our friends listened to the story totally engaged and impressed. I was amazed how easy it was for him to talk about his life, and yet how complicated it was for me to talk about myself.

He continued with the other side of the argument: "But my father wanted to do the same thing for me, and it was nonsense. For instance, ever since I finished my fourth year in medical school he has been trying to play matchmaker for his niece and me. This has been a huge challenge for the past two years and has made our relationship harsh, with my mother in the middle. I have been trying to convince him that times have changed, and it is so difficult for him to admit this. But I never give up and I know I have a choice for my own future. My parents know my future is not in their hands."

I was very curious and asked how old the niece was.

He said, "Sixteen."

"Why did you reject her?"

"Because I was looking for love."

We all laughed. So he told that couple not to give up, not to think about leaving the country, and to find a way to solve the problem.

This was a very different way than I had learned to deal with problems as a girl in a family that depended on others for support. I had learned to shut up and run away. Behrooz had the power of an independent man, raised by a man, in a male dominated society. My role models were all women who had some successes, but were often victims of the culture and circumstances.

Iran has a multi-cultural population and Iranians used to celebrate December 25th, Jesus' birthday, as a holy event. For Muslims, Jesus is considered the second prophet of Allah, coming after Moses and before Mohammad. There were also many Christians in Iran at that time. There were Christmas parties in some night clubs. Christmas and New Year's Eve were happy times for Iranians. As I remember, it almost always snowed on Christmas Eve.

Behrooz was born that same night. I invited him to a famous night club named Chattanooga. It was located on Pahlavi Avenue, the most beautiful and longest avenue in the Middle East. Iranian and American pop music were played there. First he hesitated to accept. He said he didn't like dancing, but I insisted that we go there and socialize. Finally he agreed and we went. But he couldn't take the loud music and smoky air, which made him very uncomfortable, so we left and went to Hilton Hotel's restaurant. It was a nice, quiet place on the 20th floor, with a candle lighted on each table, beautiful hanging chandeliers, a huge Christmas tree decorating the corner and relaxing jazz music. We were offered a corner table by the window. To the north, the mountains were covered with white snow. To the south, the view of Tehran's roads, trees, buildings and icy lights made an unforgettable scene—distant and lovely. We ordered dinner and the waiter asked if we wanted to order wine.

I said, "I don't drink."

But I was dying to have one. I knew culturally it was not acceptable for a girl to drink alcohol, especially at a restaurant. Behrooz ordered one glass of Shiraz wine for himself.

While we were waiting to order, he held my hand and said, "I want to have you forever." I always got teased by my friends because I am so romantic and maybe belonged in the 18th century. Now here I'm so grateful that I found someone that belongs to the 18th century too.

I said, "I feel the same for you." I was so shy to say, 'I love you'.

He said, "I want to hear from you that you love me."

I said, "I wrote to you."

Behrooz said as his birthday present, he wanted me to say it so he could hear it.

My heart was pounding and I was suffocating.

Finally I said it in a very soft voice, and he made me repeat it louder and louder, then he teased me and said, "Are you the same girl that told me she is a gambler, dancer and speed driver?" He said I was hiding myself behind that false character I pretended to be.

"You are still a puzzle to me."

That night he proposed.

When I went to nursing school, I had made a plan to work and study very hard for six years in order to relieve my mother of her demanding life in which she had been trapped for so many years to save her children. Then, after these six years, I would apply for immigration to America, and take my mother with me to live free from all of the cultural prejudices—the cruel and snobbish society that branded her. For this reason, right after my graduation I sent my documentation to different hospitals in the US and got a good job offer in Brooklyn Methodist Hospital. I was waiting to finish my contract with the University Hospital to pay my school debt. I did not have any desire to live forever in Iran. I have always loved Iran, the country, but had always railed against a culture where women are still oppressed. Unfortunately, I found that that it is not only true in Iran, but even in my new homeland of America.

Since Behrooz and I started dating, I realized I wanted a man in my life, but not so close that he would interfere with my long-range plan. Our romantic relationship was extremely dear to me, but I wanted things to continue the way they were. I had a personal goal with which marriage couldn't compare. But I loved Behrooz so much that I didn't want to lose him. How was I going to respond to this situation? What were my survival options?

When I didn't react to his proposal with exuberance, Behrooz sensed that something was terribly wrong.

He asked, "What is going on? You don't seem excited at all. Your reaction doesn't make any sense!"

I said, "I AM very excited, but I am also quite afraid. You are moving so fast and I am not ready yet."

He said with a tone of disappointment, "Are you saying no?"

"Of course not. I want you in my life for ever, but please understand me. I need more time. This is a very important moment in my life. I need you by my side, but please don't rush."

He was very confused, and asked, "How much more time are

you talking about? And what will be different later?"

I said, "I don't know. I am very worried. If you believe me, you shouldn't get upset."

"What do you want me to do? Just tell me what to do." responded Behrooz.

I tried to cheer him up. "Nothing is wrong. I just need more time."

Again, he asked, "Time for what? We are two adults and we are acting like sixteen year old Romeo and Juliet. I am doing my best to make us enjoy our lives and grow closer together. Do you love me? Is your family pushing you with a prearranged marriage?"

I wished those were my problems. With my rebellious spirit those were easy to solve. My problem was my huge responsibility for my mother's life. I told him the problem was not what he thought. I envied his freedom. I didn't share my feelings with him. It was easier for me to be quiet and pretend the proposal had never been made.

He seemed hurt and very tense, shaking one leg with agitation, fidgeting with his shirt buttons and moving his cup from one place to another on the table. While we were sitting there, we both were uncomfortable. For a while we listened to the live music, each preoccupied with our own thoughts. I eventually became so irritated with the music that I suggested we leave. On the way home, he drove with one hand and held my hand gently with the other. He drove very slowly, lost in thought and sighing occasionally.

I put my head on his shoulder. I was dying for him, but I didn't want to get closer.

I was imagining the married people I knew and realized that it was now possible for me to make a choice to be married.

Until this moment, marriage had been illustrated through a series of very unhappy women's experiences, connected to their family relationships and circumstances. I imagined that if we got closer, his family would become nosy and would look disparagingly down on my mother and my family. Then I'd lose him and my life would be ruined.

As we rode in silence, my mom's stepmother's (Bibi's) voice was running through my mind like a record player. She was telling Mom, "You ruined your father's reputation by being a servant. You even were incapable of being a prostitute to make a better life for you and your children. Why didn't you put your children in a foster home to get married with Dr. Vaziri?"

My mom's stepmother was vicious; she put down my mother in the worst possible way. Shame and guilt overwhelmed me with these thoughts. I felt I had been emotionally frozen.

That evening I spent with him would be any girl's dream, but for me it was wrenching. Both my dream and my nightmare came true at the same moment. When we reached home, he stopped the car and followed me to the door.

He said "I remember the first day in the operating room, how scared you were. Don't worry. You'll be OK. And I will do my best to make you happy and I would never leave you no matter what."

Then he left. I was relieved.

All night I thought through the possibility that he, Mom and I would eventually go to America, and all these worries about family intervention would be overcome. He had already passed his test, and so was available to leave right away.

The day after was Friday and we both were off from work. When we saw each other he anxiously asked, "How do you feel today? Did you think more about us?"

I said, "Yes, we both are only twenty-two years old, we have lots of time ahead of us."

He interrupted, "Are you kidding me? We can't continue like this. Our relationship is like a cat and mouse game. I want us to have a serious relationship. I wish to get closer to you. I respect our culture; I just want a decent and normal adult relationship. The love, the passion is here between us, but I don't understand your problem at all. We are playing reverse roles. Usually, girls want to marry right away and the guy is not ready. Now when I propose to you, you want me to wait. Unless you don't love me, or are waiting for some other guy, why won't you agree to marry me? Please be honest with me."

I started to cry.

I said, "I have lots of responsibilities. You are a free person, but I have a different life than you. I feel like I am drowning and taking you down with me. It is not fair to saddle you with my problems. It is not you that creates the problem. I am terribly concerned about people judging my mother's and my life."

And then I told him my many concerns and worries, and my wish to leave the country with him and Mom.

He said, "Look at you. Since last night when I proposed you look sick and drained. This is not a big problem and we can overcome it when you calm down and think rationally about it. If you want to leave the country, I have passed the ESFMG test and even though I did not plan to leave the country, it is possible. Your mom is no problem. You overvalue other people's judgment. Who cares what they think?"

It was snowing; we were walking arm in arm. I cried quietly

and couldn't stop my tears. I was wearing a hat with a matched wool shawl; the front of the shawl was drenched with tears. I just wanted to stop time and not let it move on. We walked a very long distance around Tehran University, our favorite walkway.

Later that afternoon he took me to the Tehran City Hall Theater to see the Nutcracker that was presented as a Christmas event by a group from Norway. The happy atmosphere, watching the lively ballet and hearing the beautiful violin music, washed all my hurt feelings away. I held his hand tightly and felt safe and secure again. My heart was lightened and the wondering was gone. I felt as light as that ballerina.

Later he said, "My sister is coming from America for my graduation and my parents planned a graduation party." He wanted to surprise his family by introducing me to them as his fiancé on the same evening.

I said, "This is not a good way to start. They are going to be offended; they will be angry from the beginning.

He said we'd give our families this chance later, but this was our lives and we had a right to make our own decision without any interference. We were old enough to do that. "You know you are not the only one under your family's pressure. I have my own problem with parents! My father wants me to marry his niece, and I obviously don't have any intention of following his plan."

I realized he was trapped too.

Then he continued, "My stepfather thinks my mother owes him a favor, because when she was a widow and pregnant, he married her and adopted me. So now he wants some compensation!"

Oh my God, that was why he understood my terrified feelings and thoughts so well. I felt so self-centered and preoccupied with myself, because I never got closer to him and let him talk about himself.

He said, "Let's do as you said and not talk about anything but love. You didn't realize that when you made a deal not to talk about our families, that you freed me from my strained situation, as well as your own. We'll find a way!"

It was January fourteenth, the night before his stepsister's arrival. He took me to Shah-Abdulazim, a holy place in the south of Tehran that was not a typical place for a date. This was a holy place where people went to pray and seek guidance from God for their problems. We were sitting in the car and watching the gold and mosaic tomb, all illuminated with green lights as if God was sitting right there with all His brightness and glory, watching us. I watched him with surprise as he started to pray. "God help us be strong and resolute in our decision." Then he took my hands and asked me to repeat after him:

"Thank you, God, for the gift of love between us. We will be together with heartfelt gratitude forever. We will stay together and support each other forever, no matter who or what might try to interfere. God, please fill our hearts to overflow with trust and passion and shower us with your blessing."

Then we both promised God, "We do."

He passed me a delicate, beautiful engagement ring, and joked, "You owe me one."

In this moment we broke with our culture, and emblazoned a new, rebellious path together. This type of ceremony, called *segheh*, was accepted for temporary marriage for older people or those who want to hide their marriage, even for men to have another woman behind their wife's back; but not for educated people like us. However, we were both very independent and didn't need any witnesses, intervention or legal papers to announce our love.

That moment was tattooed in my mind forever, although I knew if this secret ceremony was ever revealed it would ruin my reputation for the future and in the modern society that we lived. It was not respected at all, but I had no doubt in my mind to trust him. I'd be ready for any and all consequences.

I felt as if I was in heaven.

It was the day after, January 15, 1969—a bright, icy day. Everywhere was covered with snow and icicles sparkled in the brilliant sunlight. I felt as though it was nature's wedding day. I was invited to Behrooz's graduation party tonight. I was looking for the most beautiful dress that I could find. Finally I borrowed an elegant black velvet dress with a short skirt, long sleeves and diamond buttons from a friend. I wore suede, black, high heeled shoes. I pulled my long hair up and fixed it in Audrey Hepburn's style. And I sprayed half of my Nina Ricci perfume bottle all over my body. My heart was shining like my little diamond engagement ring that matched the buttons on my friend's dress.

I looked into the mirror over and over again until my mom stepped into my room and said, "Oh, my, you look so beautiful! Where are you going?"

I said, "My friend is coming from the United States, and invited me to a party. Don't worry; I'm going to be late."

She used to pray with her hands turned inward and then blew the prayer into your face to take the devil away and make things easier for you. Later she got her visa at the American embassy in Turkey this way, by charming the officer with her good prayers. Just now, she spread her prayers over me.

At 6 PM, I took a taxi to the place that Behrooz always waited for me. He was so happy that he was nearly jumping out of his skin. He came toward me and admired my look and my dress. When you are in love, you already have tacit approval, so he was happy on top of happy. We went towards his small car. He opened the door for me and kissed my hand and I slid into my seat. When he moved into the car, he looked at me again and whistled. It made me laugh.

Then he said, "You are my beautiful jasmine flower."

He started the car and began to drive. On our way he sometimes stopped the car and told me how much he loved me. I was shy and quiet, but my insides were blooming with a heavenly blossom, beautiful and hot as fire. I was so emotional that I could hardly keep from crying. I told him that I felt so lucky, that I was afraid to even say it out loud because I might lose it.

And he said, "Nothing, nothing can separate us. I promise."

I said, "But I feel like there is a storm in my heart."

He took my hand and teased me, "Please don't faint at my house like you did in the operating room!"

We both laughed. He said, "I talked a lot about you with my mother. She is my mentor, and she encouraged me to go after you. She said true love was rare and you should follow your heart."

Still, I was nervous.

When we arrived, he introduced me as his fiance. His mother hugged and kissed me; his stepfather seemed cold but welcomed me. This made me calm. All my nervousness was gone. Behrooz looked at me with his perfect smile and winked.

It was a simple but elegant dinner table, with a handmade tablecloth, napkins, two matching, antique crystal candlesticks with white candles, and a low, oval vase with red and white roses floating in water.

His mother said, "White flowers are Behrooz's favorite."

Behrooz, who was very funny around his parents, said she knew that for sure, and I smiled.

After dinner we sat—Behrooz, me, his mom and step-father—and Behrooz went to make us tea. His mom asked if I had any brothers or sisters.

I said, "No brother, but two sisters."

She said, "I have Behrooz and a younger daughter, one year younger than him, and she will arrive at midnight for her brother's graduation."

Then she told me how much she missed her daughter. She related how she lost Behrooz's father when she was two months pregnant. Then she pointed to her husband and said, "Hujee, my husband is his stepfather."

His stepfather said, "Behrooz is my soul. I couldn't live without him."

Behrooz was anxious to stop his stepfather from going any further. "Let me show her the house and our family's pictures. I want her to see my sister's picture and to recognize her at the airport before we introduce her."

Hujee-Agha seemed unfinished with his investigation, but Behrooz's mom said, "It's 9 PM so you guys make sure to make it to Mehr-Abad airport by 11 o'clock."

Behrooz showed me around the house. It was a small duplex

with a nice, bright sitting room, a square dining room with a huge mirror in which I watched myself as though in some romantic movie and a kitchen with a wash room down stairs. We went upstairs. Upstairs there were three bedrooms and a shower. His room was facing Elizabeth Boulevard, a famous avenue close to the hospital.

I teased him, "That's why you were always on time to work."

He seemed very happy and excited. He said, "Did you see how much my mother liked you? She couldn't take her eyes away from you. When you went to the bathroom, she highly admired my choice. I can't wait for my sister to meet you. She already knows you through my letters and I already sent her your picture."

In his room, he brought his family album over and started kissing my hands and face and said, "I was dying for this moment to be alone with you. Nine months is a long time to wait."

It was the best feeling of pureness and passion, and he just didn't want to let me go. I was trying to change the situation by telling him that we would be late for the airport. He was trying to get closer to me. He was trying to push me towards the bed by telling me how much he had waited for this moment.

I said, "Wait! We are not married yet."

He said, "Relax, we are engaged now. Remember we went to that holy place and we promised each other to be together for ever?"

I said, "That deals with our feelings, but we have to go through the ritual ceremony."

He said, "We will. I'll do whatever you want."

He kissed me and said, "I can't wait anymore. I am tired of waiting. Please, show me your love. Don't act childish. Why is it so hard for you to get closer to me?"

When he gently pulled me close to him, I was thinking that this was what we both wanted, and couldn't understand why I didn't just take it easy—this is my dear beloved Behrooz, my fiancé. I took off my long hanging earrings and put them on the bed stand.

Then I noticed the large picture on the bed stand. Although I had only seen the man once in my life, I immediately recognized the photo as my father, Rasoul.

Oh my God, we have the same father. And I screamed, from deep in my throat, "STOP, stop, that is my father's picture!"

"No! That's my father's picture!"

"Your father? He's outside!!"

"No this is my real father in the picture. Why are you afraid of a simple picture? Don't worry, it's gone." He turned the picture face down on the table. "The man in the other room is my father."

"No, this is the picture of my father—not yours. My older sister has this picture."

He was shocked. He looked at me like I was crazy; he started to scream, broke the mirror with his fist, blood started to flow. He kicked the nightstand and threw the picture against the door, smashing the frame and glass. He was screaming and swearing to God. Everyone in the party ran to see what was going on.

His stepfather came and put his hand on my forehead and asked what was going on. And I said, "Your son is my brother."

I stayed motionless and numb the whole night. I heard the whispers and talking, going and coming, but I was still. They picked up his sister from the airport. His mother was taken to the hospital in emotional distress. His father tried to help me as much as possible. Behrooz was coming and going, as his father related this story that I had already heard from my mother:

"When this man in the picture was involved in politics and when he was trying to escape from the country, he ran to the dead end valley. He hid from the police in an abandoned house. The owner of the house gave him safe harbor, hiding him from the police and military. During the time he was hiding, he had an affair with the owner's unmarried daughter. When he escaped again, and finally made his way to Russia, she was pregnant with Behrooz. When he escaped he never came back, we thought he was dead in the war."

I said, "No, he is alive."

His father put me in the car and we went to Aki's house. As soon as Aki saw me and Behrooz's stepfather she said, "Oh, my poor sister, have you been in an accident? What happened to you?"

I asked to lie down somewhere and for her to bring our father's picture out. She was surprised and said I always hated that picture. I said I still hated the picture but show it to me anyway.

We compared Aki's picture with the picture from the stepfather's case. They matched. And that was the end of my love life.

In the garden, I watch a huge colony of ants. They are running around and some of them carry miniature objects, but much bigger than themselves. Some are dead under the steps. A group of them work together to carry the dead bodies away. What are they thinking? What are they feeling? Are they chanting something in sorrow? My heart aches as I listen to the spirit of the moment and I hear the poet, Khalil Gibran:

> "Your pain is the breaking of the shell that encloses your
> understanding.
> Even as the stone of the fruit must break, that its heart may
> stand in the sun, so must you know pain.
> And could you keep your heart in wonder at the daily miracles
> of your life, your pain would not seem less wondrous than
> your joy;
> And you would accept the seasons of your heart, even as you
> have always accepted the seasons that pass over your fields.
> And you would watch with serenity through the winters of
> your grief."

It took me that winter and spring of grieving for my beloved brother and lost relationship before I could move on. For six months, the whole world seemed cruel and unfair. I was torn apart and in an extremely private despair, because it was hard to share this with anyone. I didn't know if anybody could understand and whether they would judge me. I missed Behrooz terribly, not knowing whether I mourned more for such an intelligent, perfect brother that I always dreamed of or the tender passionate love of a soul mate. This incident was like a tornado tearing my identity apart—I could feel my brain, body and feelings scattered and separated from one another.

During the day I worked very hard, and during the night I was like a body without a soul, cold and numb. My soul wandered through the trees, mountains, everywhere again. All philosophy and beliefs became meaningless. So many times I imagined Behrooz as a brother, going with him to take care of my mother, having a man beside me. A moment later he was the same person bringing me flowers in the hospital, writing poems and wishing to marry me. I would die each morning to get up and see that my nightmare was real. I opened a file in my mind and put this memory in a dark, hidden corner where I became increasingly afraid to approach or open it. It was so well hidden that I didn't open it for 30 years.

I stopped seeing the people we both knew and tried to find a new life. To recover and start over, I returned to my high school friends with whom I had partied a lot and with whom life was more superficial. My closest friend was Shahla, a very popular girl who knew lots of people. Her father and uncle were in the ministry of the Shah's government and had lots of parties. She and her brothers and sisters were smart, outgoing, and fun people. I returned to my old habits, hiding under the shadow of their world. I also had friends from the university, Mehry, who had been my roommate, and her friend Abbass, who she later married. They had a wonderful community of friends—newly graduated nurses and doctors who enjoyed being together, took trips to the north of Iran, and had joyful and playful gatherings. In this group was also Gretel, a beautiful Christian girl who was our third roommate. So I had two different groups that I spent time with—one from high school and one from the university.

The university group was modern in the sense that we "hung out together," but not as boyfriend or girlfriend. The high school group was very interesting because they had real fun. They were mostly rich and traveled outside the country, bringing ideas from many cultures back to Iran. They usually paired off. There was a daughter of Professor Adle, named Katherine (Katty), whose mom was French and father was a very famous orthopedic doctor who was one of the Shah's doctors and gambling buddies. Katty was paralyzed after a horse fall; she was beautiful and kind and was the girlfriend of Shahla's brother, Bahman. Through Katty we were often at high society parties, and the first time Shahla introduced me to Katty we became fast friends. I was invited to these parties through both of these girls. After about six months, during the summer, Bahman held a surprise birthday party for Katty at her farm far from Tehran. This was a huge party—Princess Shahnaz (the Shah's daughter), who was now divorced, arrived with her boyfriend in a helicopter—very unusual for 1970. The gift table rivaled a boutique store window or famous showroom. I wondered if all of this helped Katty deal with sitting in a wheelchair for the rest of her life, if she was really enjoying this day; but I could see pain in Katty's eyes and knew that the opulence gave her no pleasure. Shahla's brother, Bahman, who was about 23 years old and very handsome, tall with green eyes and uninterested in education, really loved Katty. The only thing that really made her happy was this handsome, free soul who people used to call "the Elvis Presley of Iran." He even dressed, sang and acted like him.

At this party, one of the guests, Fariborz, was playing guitar and singing the songs of Aref, a famous Iranian musician. Aref was my favorite singer. Fariborz didn't normally choose to sing at social occasions, but he was a close friend of Katty and he knew he soothed her heart with his gift of a song. Most of the partygoers were couples, but I was alone with myself. I went closer and my passion for the music and song made me dissolve into the performance. Old me disappeared into the music and a new me was born.

These parties repeated and I saw Fariborz more. On Shahla's birthday, Katty offered to hold the party at her place and invited Fariborz as a birthday gift. Shahla called in advance and said that Fariborz was coming, and she made a point to say that he was 'very interested' in me. She wanted me to be aware, so if I was interested I could take the appropriate action.

I was starting to feel alive again, and happy. I dressed nicely in a green dress with a full skirt, fitted top and high heeled, black shoes. Shahla gave me a ride to the party and on the ride Bahman was driving and singing. We talked and laughed all the way, joking about what a good match Fariborz and I were together. When we arrived, Fariborz was sitting shyly by his guitar, formally and conservatively dressed, absorbed in himself. He approached me and invited me to sit by him. I was a little shy, too, because he was the singer in the performing group and a lot of attention was showered on him by the girls.

There were two types of music—tango and waltz, and then hippie music, Elvis and the Beatles. I thought back to my child-hood experiences with that music, when I was always in the corner observing. Now I was at the heart of the music, honored by the best singer and feeling inside of the group. Fariborz and I danced the tango and waltz. He sang a famous Iranian song, *Me-sal-e-toor-e-mahi-ha*, which had my nickname, Mahi, and honored me in this way. The guests loved it.

After this party, Fariborz asked me out and, although I was working very hard and didn't have lots of time, we went out occasionally. When I was emotionally ready, I got involved with him. He told me he was in his last year of a pharmacology degree program at Tehran University. His father had a drug store on Pahlavi Avenue and he planned to work there after graduation. In my mind, I wondered why he didn't plan to go abroad but he assured me that because he had a family business and all his family were pharmacists, he could make a good living in Tehran. Until now everything pointed to a future abroad, but now Fari-borz's strong commitment showed me a possible alternative. I started to imagine the future through his lens, without aban-doning Iran. It could be possible to be secure and successful in Iran. I was desperate to go to America, but couldn't leave because of my mother. He had a father to support him and I began to envision a future in Iran with him. I could see a path where I could stay and have my mother and my life together.

In almost a year of this relationship, he showed me lots of passion, love and respect. He took me to very expensive restaurants and shows, always gave me gifts of perfume and I wondered how I could ever repay all this kindness. I wondered if I had the pedigree to match this man's expectations. It took me six months to accept Fariborz as a trusted friend and potential future fiancé. I invited him to meet Mehry, Khosro (Mehry's brother)and my university friends and together we enjoyed them and they enjoyed him. Time passed and I started to feel love again. We were a couple that everyone saw with a future together—more serious than friends.

The Iranian New Year, called *Nouroz* which means 'New Day', is celebrated on the first day of spring. Iranians believe when Nouroz comes your life starts again like you are reborn. As all the green and life comes back to nature, you also can bring yourself back to a new life, change and start all over again. I had a plan to change my life. You grow and change along with the tulips, hyacinths and Grecian windflowers.

At the holiday of New Year's (the 13th day of the Iranian New Year) there was a huge celebration. I took Fariborz out with our other friends and we were in a tenant garden outside of the city having a picnic. The whole day I thought that I would ask Fariborz what he had in mind for the future. With my experience I had the wisdom to think ahead and set expectations and not play around. I made a plan to ask him directly what his intentions were. He was talking about everything except plans for engagement and marriage.

We were playing football and running around a lot that day and I got tired, so I sat down and he started to walk over to me.

Suddenly in a beautiful sign of spring, a butterfly that had been flitting about settled right on my head. Fariborz kept coming toward me.

When I asked what he was doing, he said, "Nothing I am just after the butterfly."

Then he said in a low and sad voice, "I wish you were so easy to capture as this butterfly."

I asked "What do you mean? Why do you sound so sad?"

He said, "Things are not as easy as you think. You know I am Jewish."

"Katty told me when you asked me out and I already told my mother. Mom said, 'Thank God he is not a communist—at least he has a God!'"

Fariborz said, "You don't mind?"

I told him, "Who cares?"

He said, "It's not easy with my family. I knew this relationship would not end well."

I asked, "Why not?"

He said, "My parents have arranged a Jewish girl for me and my father is totally against you and me together. My children will not be Jewish unless they are born to a Jewish woman, and my father told me if I marry outside of the Jewish faith, I will lose my heritage—drug store, wealth, family—I will have to leave."

I looked at him in disbelief. How did I not see this selfish, mommy-boy in him? Why didn't he tell me sooner? How could he play with my life like this?

I hollered at him, "What kind of person do you think I am? Why did you continue seeing me? Why did you write a song about me? Why did you sing all those romantic songs to me? What was in your dirty mind? If you cared about religion, why didn't you go out with a Jewish girl and leave me alone?" I gathered some dirt from the ground and threw it in his face. I told him I hated him. I ran toward Mehry, her brother Khosro and the group of friends standing around Sharhrokh's car listening to music playing on the car's tape player. Sharhrokh, Khosro's nephew, was very outgoing and a happy provider—he was the life of the party.

They stood there and I climbed on the roof of the car, lay down and closed my eyes. My mind compared this religious attack, this time from a Jew, to others from the clergy in the past, and reminded me that I had to shut up and run away. The sun was burning my face, and the heat from the car metal soaked deep into my body like a heating pad, easing my pain and infusing me with warmth like nurturing arms. But I knew I was once again alone in this world.

Bahman's father was a womanizer who was very hard on his children. He was like an army officer, ordering his children around and making very tough rules. No matter what the children did, it wasn't enough. Bahman's older brother became an officer in the army, following his father's steps. Bahman and his sister Shahla, the two middle children, became rebels. The youngest boy left Iran forever to America. Bahman and Katty, two rebels with injuries—one emotional and one physical—bonded together and soothed the pain with their love. In the last two years of their lives, they also found comfort through religion, creating an inner, personal revolution against the secular society. They became fundamentally involved with their own beliefs. Katty started to wear a chador and they grew self sufficient, growing their own food, isolating themselves in a fenced compound with a few people from the village. In the meantime, Bahman carved a cave into the hillside near the farmhouse to hide arms for the fight for the end of the world.

Dr. Adle disowned his daughter when she married and went this extreme religious way. Through all their prayers, surprisingly, God gave Bahman and Katty a very beautiful little girl—a miracle for Katty who never expected to be able to have a child. They named her Fatima, and she reinforced their beliefs even further.

The birth of this child changed their way of life. They became extremely religious. They disconnected themselves from most of our friends. They moved to the village of Khoramdareh, and lived among the poor villagers. Bahman let his beard and hair grow long. He dressed like a farmer and wore a green headband. Through his hard work with the farmers his skin turned a leathery dark brown. Katty spent her money to help the village's poor people. Bahman and Katty impressed me deeply, and they often invited me to the village as a community nurse to help the needy. I loved this work.

Bahman believed himself to be a holy messenger coming from Mohammad's side, and Katty followed him faithfully. Eventually, they went to the mountains in Khoram-Dareh, west of Tehran, and lived in the cave but also built and lived in a house nearby. They made their home into a holy place, wrote quotes from the Qur'an on the walls, and Bahman brought another two girls, Mariam and Masumeh, children from a previous marriage, to this life. So Katty and her daughter lived with Bahman and two other daughters almost three years. I used to see them occasionally, and was amused by their fast, unusual change from Elvis Presley and parties to beards and Qur'an. The Shah threatened to disown his daughter because she joined this cause with Katty and Bahman, even though she was not so devout. His daughter stayed away publicly, but still stayed in touch. Bahman and Katty became more and more dangerous to the Shah and the government of Iran, as they advertised and criticized the Shah's misdeeds. Bahman had a list of all the top ministers to be assassinated in order to make a pure society for Muslims.

After three years, the newspapers and populace became aware of them and the SAVAK began to watch them closely. Although Bahman and Katty were not involved with any larger group, they were still considered a threat. So one day the SAVAK came in force and surrounded their home. It was all over the newspaper, radio and TV. But Bahman had left Katty and the children in the cave with food, water and weapons and he managed to escape to Tehran with his list of enemies, heavily armed, to commit jihad and save Islam.

The SAVAK found out about the cave, surrounded the opening and told Katty to come out. But she refused. So a negotiator came to the mouth of the cave and read a plea from her father asking her to leave this way of life, saying that he would take care of her.

Katty announced from the cave, "No way. I have found my way and this is the way God wants me to be."

And she shot the SAVAK negotiator in the head. And then the SAVAK shot Katty in the head.

There were devastating pictures in the news of the three children, 9, 7 and 3 years old, who were horrified, but survived. Bahman hid in Tehran, but was found by the SAVAK, who were expert at tracking and finding their enemies. They assassinated him in his hiding place.

It was a sunny, warm Friday. The news shouted from newspapers, radio and television that Bahman and Katty were assassinated.

Normally, they would have left his body where it was shot to rot. But because of his uncle, General Hojat who held a high government role, they put his body in the trunk of the car and returned it to his parent's house.

A black Cadillac parked in front of the house. Two very well-dressed strong agents wearing black suits, white shirts and red ties politely came to the door and asked for Bahman's father. When he answered they talked for a short time and then they opened the trunk and revealed Bahman's bullet-riddled body to the family. Everyone started to cry.

When she saw the body, Shahla screamed deep from her heart, "Oh, my young handsome brother!"

Bahman's mom queried, "Why did this happen to you, Bahman? You were such a happy boy. What changed you and brought you to this end? What is going to happen to your three daughters now?

Bahman's uncle, who was pro-Shah, and the regime, said, "This is black restitution for the young Muslims who oppose the Shah. Bahman has paid the price for his actions and those of his comrades."

Bahman's father, a womanizer who had been absent during his children's childhood and abdicated their moral education to others, agreed with the uncle and his face showed his sadness and guilt, but he put up a good, strong front for the other men around.

I got angry, "This is not the time to speak of Bahman's beliefs and judge him. Be sensitive to what you say in front of his dead body and loving family."

Khosro and I had come to support and help Shahla and her parents in this devastating situation. Most of their friends and family were there. Secret police were swarming all over. Everyone was afraid to show any emotion, except those who were pro-regime. They partied amongst themselves, talking about daily issues, eating, drinking and even sometimes joking and laughing. Some were quietly sitting sadly, lost deep in their own thoughts, but this was dangerous.

We had all been terrified, confused, and deeply saddened by the dramatic turns in Katty and Bahman's lives. Now we understood why and we were confronted with the dangers of this radical belief in Islam and the difficulties of their family situation.

I thought, "No wonder Bahman and Katty isolated themselves from this conflicted family. I sat there and cried hopelessly, remembering the day Katty hugged her baby and celebrated, "I have a baby, this is a pure miracle! Thank you, God."

I thought of Bahman, that happy boy playing guitar , imitating Elvis.

I thought of my murdered Uncle Reza, of Behrooz who thought his father was murdered, of my own refugee father, Rasoul, and on...and on.

Khosro came over, took my hand, and led me to the balcony. Having Khosro there was a blessing.

He said, "Look at you. You look so broken. I understand how difficult this is for you, this terribly sad day. I know how close you are to this family." Tears appeared in his eyes and rolled down his cheeks, giving me permission to let loose the floodgates of feelings. I wept, and he tried to calm me down.

He said, "Bahman and Katty acted destructively. I believe the Shah's regime acted cruelly, as usual. But Bahman and Katty did not belong to any ensemble, any organization, no leader, no group plan. They immaturely acted on their own, to fulfill their own desires. They didn't even think of their innocent children. Did these children have any choice not to be in this horrible situation?"

I thought, "He is right. Politics and beliefs are not more important than your children; even rebels need to think ahead and be organized about their lives."

Then he said, "Bahman had a lot of energy and power, and Katty had lots of money. They could have expressed their disagreement in a civilized way and do something for the nation and country."

I asked, "So you judge them? You think they were crazy!?"

He said, "I don't judge them at all. I wish they had been more mature. Remember you can not be emotional about politics. Political action needs planning and leadership.

This was exactly the opposite of Behrooz, who didn't care about politics and thought no one should act politically, and that we should leave the politicians alone and live our own lives. I cared about politics, and now was learning that involvement in politics could be something organized, and that I could be a part without being alone.

The Ambulance came to take Bahman to the cemetery. Bahman's mother went toward Bahman's covered body laid out on a stretcher. She was devastated and cried…hitting herself on the face, scratching her skin and holding the stretcher in an effort not to let go of his soul.

She cried, "What am I going to do without you? No, no, don't leave me, Bahman, the light of my eyes. Don't go. Why, why, why?"

All the guests stared to cry. I held back my tears, and helped her sit on a nearby chair, momentarily surprised that I had reverted to my nursing nature and could control my emotions. Her nephew was a doctor and gave her an shot of valium which put her to sleep and soothed her pain.

When she was numbed, I burst into tears. It was difficult for me, too, to let Bahman and Katty go. Khosro was very concerned about me. He took my hand and we all went to the cemetery. Although Khosro mentioned his disapproval of Bahman's rebellious nature, he was deeply saddened as well, and helped the family like his own family. He respected Bahman like a brother.

The funeral was under control of the secret police, which ordered everyone around and directed every movement. People were very cautious to show no emotion. When we arrived in the cemetery, as is Muslim tradition, Khosro carried Bahman's body to the private washing area and prayed out loud while washing Bahman's body . He bravely showed the wounded areas of the body to the men who were witnessing this ritual, as a silent political act which he hoped would allow the news of this tragedy to reach the public.

The rule is that to capture someone, the SAVAK must shoot them in the foot. There was no wound in Bahman's feet but three gunshot holes in the head, and two in his chest. Everyone was now a witness.

Bahman's body was buried and the soil, the heart of the earth, embraced his torn body to comfort him forever. We did not see or know how Katty departed to the earth.

We tried to calm Shahla and her parents down, but they were understandably inconsolable. This story had great impact for the people of Tehran, and was a cultural tragedy as well as a personal one. The most modern and happy of my friends lived lives that ended in tragedy. My rebel soul was very close to their souls, but they changed faster than I could.

Bahman's two daughters were taken by their uncle, Bahman's

younger brother, and later brought to the United States. Princess Shahnaz, the daughter of the Shah who also had one daughter, adopted Katty's daughter Fatima, and before the revolution they left the country and now live in France.

In the garden I think of all the beauty of Katty and Bahman. Their free lives, their laughter, how this Elvis transformed into a messenger and then was killed this way?

> *Yet the timeless in you is aware of life's timelessness,*
> *And knows that yesterday is but today's memory and*
>   *tomorrow is today's dream.*
> *And that that which sings and contemplates in you is still*
>   *dwelling within the bounds of that first moment which*
>   *scattered the stars into space.*

—*Kahlil Gibran*

When I cut away the damaged flowers in the garden, I still remember each bloom's beauty and fragrance, but there is room for others to grown.

ne hot summer day at the beginning of my friendship with Mehry, she invited me to her house for
lunch. Aghdas, her older sister, joined us—she
looked like a beautiful, sexy movie star. I thought,
"No wonder Mehry looks so gorgeous. We called her Ava Gardner
at school. Both sisters were tall and elegant, with astonishing black
hair and eyes. Her mom was immensely beautiful and sweet, and
the family called her Brigit Bardot. She was a fabulous cook and
made us a delicious lunch. She was a relaxed and happy woman
who made me feel very comfortable.

As I arrived, they hugged me and welcomed me saying, "Here
you are! We heard a lot about you from Mehry. She is very fond of
you and talks of you often."

I said, "If you come to my house, then you will learn how
much my family loves her as well."

Later Khosro and his older brother, Houshang and their
nephew, Sharhrokh, joined us. When I saw them, I was surprised
at how beautiful and handsome each individual was. They each
seemed special-ordered from God! I couldn't help myself and the
thought formed words and spilled out of my mouth!

"Mehry! Do you have your father's picture?"

She asked, "Why?"

I said, "Because all of your family looks like models, and I think that your father must have looked like Omar Sharif."

We all laughed. She showed me her deceased father's picture. I was right!

That day we played cards, joked a lot and enjoyed each others' company. Khosro didn't play with us. He was sitting in a corner of the room, busy with his own work, but I realized he was watching me stealthily.

When I was leaving, Khosro handed me a drawing. It was a portrait of me.

In front of everybody he said, "You are very beautiful. You have a baby's soft colored skin and an angel's face. I flushed and escaped to a taxi. That portrait was signed and dated by him, and I keep it to this day.

Khosro was very sensitive like me and read my feelings well. He knew when I was happy or sad. Sometimes he even came to see me at the hospital where I worked. He was ten days younger than me and I always considered him like my little brother. I loved him dearly. I cried a lot on his shoulder. I complained to him about Fariborz, and he helped me understand how it was better for me not to have this cultural clash. He made me comfortable by keeping honorable boundaries. He had an easy-going view of the world with a happy soul. We talked about every aspect of my life, except Behrooz, who I never mentioned to him or anybody. He told me that he lost his father when he was 3 years old. We built a relationship through the shared experience of growing up with our mothers only, who had both lost their husbands very young. But Khosro's father left enough money behind so his wife and children lived reasonably when he died. He recalled the story of his father's life, as it had been told to him. His father had lived in a tribe in *Pars* (old Persia). The Ghashghaei tribe waged a war with the Shah's father's army, and when they were defeated, the Reza Shah expelled them to different parts of the country without any money or support. They were mostly women, because most of the men were killed, and they lived in camps. Khosro's father, who was the only man in his family, started his own business at 19 years old. He made a good life for himself and his extended family through hand work making wooden screens, an honest business ethic. He passed away at 42 years old, a well respected citizen.

Khosro and I talked about politics and went to secret underground political meetings at Tehran University. Where Behrooz served my romantic heart very well, Khosro fed my political needs. I talked to him, learned from him and we shared common beliefs that made us soul mates. He also was my confessor—whatever I did in my life, I could use his shoulder to cry on, or to get absolved. Without a car we used to walk for miles or take the bus together everywhere. We were so simple, and we were at the same social level, which was very comfortable. For six years, we were like brother and sister.

Sharhrokh, Khosro's nephew, passed the entrance exam to go to college in England and planned to leave the country soon. He was three years younger than Khosro and me, but we three enjoyed each other's company. Khosro was a very smart, hard working student, busily writing the first Iranian computer manual. Whenever there was a party and I wanted company, Khosro advised me to go with Shahrokh. He said it was safe to go with Shahrokh, who was not only family, but a trusted friend and a well-mannered, outgoing gentleman—excellent company for a dance. Girls enviously looked at us.

The first thing I told them was, "He is my younger brother."

So with all that attention on him, we made lots of fun and got many invitations! And later we told everything to Khosro and we laughed a lot.

A week before Shahrokh left Iran for England, he asked me out alone. We went to Aria Sheraton cafeteria. As soon as we sat down, I asked him, "Why do you want to see me alone? What is wrong?"

He said, "Because I am leaving and I may not see you again, I must tell you something." My heart started to beat fast.

"Tell me! What?"

He said, "I want you to know my Uncle Khosro is deeply in love with you."

Blood rushed into my face and neck.

He laughed, "You cannot hide anything! Your face shows your embarrassment. You mean you didn't know this!?! It is so obvious to everybody around us."

I said, "No, what about Miriam? I know they were high school sweethearts."

"Who told you that?"

"I know myself. It shows. Miriam loves him."

He said, "Miriam was married a year ago; where did that thought come from? Did you ever mention this to him?"

"No, it was not my business, and he never mentioned it to me either!"

"Because he fell in love with you the first day he saw you. He always told me this."

"Oh, my God, it is six years now! Such a sneaky boy! I told him everything in my life, and he never even mentioned this!"

Shahrokh said, "Because he loves you! He wants you to choose. I told him if he waited he might lose you, Mahi, but he said, 'I am waiting for her to be mature enough to see things by herself.' He wants you to be real, and not just a dreamer."

"Oh, look at him! He is the one who is immature! He doesn't dare to tell me he loves me! Perhaps he doesn't see me as a woman! You can tell him he is very cunning, but he is just a little boy—he is just blooming!"

"No, I will tell him you love him too."

My beloved friend Shahrokh left the country in October

1969, to his own strange destiny. But he opened the door for his uncle, Khosro and me. We became romantically involved.

> *Spring comes to the garden.*
> *Ice melts.*
> *Winter, the prison of flowers, is gone.*
> *A new Nature is being born.*
> *Everything under-ground is mysteriously moving and showing*
>   *signs of Life.*
> *Earth is celebrating.*
> *I breathe pure air of heaven.*
> *Sleeping roses awaken; green carpet covers the barren soil,*
> *And Willow tree wakes up with no more feeling of loneliness.*

Khosro's sister was pregnant, and on March 12, 1971 Mehry gave birth to her first child, Sepher. Khosro came to the hospital where I was working, and when I finished my shift at 11 PM, he took me to the Jam hospital to be with Mehry during childbirth. When we got to the hospital, in the elevator, he proposed to me.

I said, "OK" right away!

So when we reached Mehry we totally surprised her with this news, and forever we celebrated Sepher's birthday and our engagement anniversary.

It is Jasmine's wedding day. Nature celebrates. The garden is full of blooms. The birds are the choir—they sing their best songs. All the frogs dance around and chant their happiness. Mother goldfish jumps up and down and cleans the pond. The big white fish baby sits with the tadpoles and tells them the story of "happily ever after." Amaryllis spreads her heavenly smell throughout the garden and all the pigeons are lazily perched on the walls, drunk from the fragrance. Grinning violets attend with colorful scarlet, canary and rosy velvet dresses. Nightingales sing antiphonally.

Oh ....I see Behrooz holding a bunch of red tulips. Oh my God! He comes toward me holding Khosro's hand...they almost reached me..

I hide myself behind the Willow tree and beg Grandfather for help. Suddenly Behrooz disappears. Khosro, with his sweet smile, reaches out to Jasmine, and the bride comes slowly to Willow tree.

She whispers to grandfather, "Willow tree, please tell me about marriage."

You are born together, and together you shall be forevermore.
You shall be together when the white wings of death scatter your days.
You shall be together even in the silent memory of God.
Give your hearts, but not into each others' keeping.
For only the hand of Life can contain your hearts.

—Kahlil Gibran

For a long time I just thought of Khosro as another friend, but over time we grew closer and more in love. We married in May, 1971, in a small, fun ceremony. It was the smallest wedding of all my friends. We could have borrowed money with a student loan to have a big wedding, but I didn't want to owe anyone. We had 40 guests, most of them friends. In one of the family houses, they made a beautiful *sofreh* for us with lots of flowers. I wore a very light, long, white wedding gown, with flowers in my hair holding a medium-length veil. My friends sprinkled a flower carpet over which we entered through the doorway and walked to the *sofreh*—most of it jasmine. I loved that. Every bride makes one wish, and I said my condition for marriage was that I didn't want to cook. Khosro said he would always hire me a cook.

The traditional Iranian ceremony took several hours in the afternoon, then after sunset we left with friends in 4 cars to a well-known sandwich shop for young people, *Yek-ta* Sandwich Shop in Tajrish. We stood by the car and each had one sandwich and one coca-cola—our big splurge. Then we went to a park and danced until midnight. To compare with all the weddings I attended—

poor or very rich—mine was the sweetest I ever attended. In the morning, for our honeymoon, Khosro and I hiked to the top of the mountain, *Tak-bagh* (singularly beautiful garden), put our things in a cave and slept out in the open. I could see the sky, the stars and moon—I think my grandmother and grandfather were there to witness me becoming a woman.

We moved into the apartment with Mom. We had both wanted a lot of children, so were delighted when Hooman was born in 1972. I got a nursing teaching job that I enjoyed and Khosro was happily working and finishing his book on computers. We eventually moved into a three bedroom apartment in a nicer area of town, and both worked hard. We bought land and, besides his job, Khosro started building our house for our future life.

We had a nanny living with us to take care of Hooman, Mom was there, Khosro's mom came to help, and we were both working hard and traveling around the world. We traveled to Japan, Thailand, and Hong Kong following Khosro's speaking engagements with IBM. The company paid for Khosro, and we paid for me to experience the world with him.

When we were married, we didn't have enough money for a wedding ring that I wanted. I chose the cheapest ring from the jewelry store at that time. In Thailand, Khosro gave me my first real wedding ring, a ruby purchased at a jewelry factory. The ruby room was just full of jewels, and I chose my ring with 5 rubies in it to represent our family and my wish for three children. Khosro bought it for me. During that trip I also bought a lot of books to take back to Iran, such as Dr. Seuss books and Fisher Price toys, and many ideas for Kindergarten, to teach my children and others. And Khosro brought back lots of ideas about computer development. We also brought back clothing—like rain I showered my family with gifts they could not afford themselves.

In 1974, we moved to another home that had more space and a yard for children to play, to prepare for another child, and to be closer to Hooman's day care center. In May, 1974 Arshia was born. He was a precious baby. These were sweet times for us. Hooman was like a father waiting for a child, taking care of me and putting things away for his brother. He saved some of his toys for the new baby. When I was 5 months pregnant, we were in a taxi that made a sharp stop. Hooman yelled at the driver that he nearly killed our baby. I wasn't showing yet, so the taxi driver asked where this baby was.

Hooman said, "It's private! It's OUR baby! It's in my mommy's tummy!"

We started to call Hooman 'The Godfather' because he was so protective.

Khosro proudly joked with Hooman, "With you taking care of Mommy, who needs me?"

I n the late '60s, when humans put the first footprints on the moon, I applied for my green card. It was so easy for doctors and nurses that the United States officials reminded me each six months to come and get it. They were anxious to have nurses and doctors because of the Vietnam War crisis. Each time they called to start the process, I postponed because I was so busy with my life, work, family and country. I didn't pay any attention until 1977. We were on a trip around the world, scheduled because Khosro was invited to an IBM meeting in Tokyo. From Japan we flew to Hawaii, they put leis around our necks, gave us our green cards, and welcomed us sweetly. It was so easy—we told the American embassy in Iran we were going to Hawaii, and they gave it to us like a driver's license. We stayed in Hawaii for two weeks, and then visited Boston to see Khosro's sister. We returned to Iran, and decided that our permanent residence would be in Iran, but that we would keep our green cards, even though it was easy to travel between Iran and the US at that time. The political relationship was fine.

Before the Revolution, Iranians did not like to leave their country. They left to go to university or to travel, but always returned home to live their lives in Iran. When Khosro got a scholarship to MIT, we decided to use our green cards to live in the U.S. until he finished. We were happy, and I was living the best life ever.

One day, we were in a crowd and I saw Behrooz from afar. I realized that I would always care for Behrooz in my heart as my brother, but that Khosro was now my love and my life. This moment of silent recognition set me free.

I n 1977 Iran, people were doing fairly well financially by the standards of the time. There were lots of opportunities, and there were no economic problems. However, people had a problem with lack of 'liberalism.' They were hungry for freedom. Since 1907, Iranians gave their blood and lives fighting for freedom of speech without censorship, free media, and the freedom to start businesses. There was a lot of corruption. Eventually, when people are well fed, they feel more deeply the starvation for individual rights. The SAVAK were secret police trained by the CIA who made life miserable for the Iranian people.

Between 1977 and 1979, there was a lot of underground activity that changed the face of Iran and the world forever. When people got frustrated and involved, there was one religious group whose leader was Ayatollah Khomeini. This group was the people's dream because they talked about a real democracy where religion would be free, women's rights would be equal to men's, and everything would be better economically, politically and religiously. He even promised that the Communists would have their own group and freedom of speech.

Iranians are devoutly religious people, and believed in the clergy deeply. At the end of 1979, the only strong, organized group who was managing the chaos was the Ayatollah Khomeini's followers. The whole country—Communists, intellectuals—all went under the Ayatollah's leadership. They all found their dreams represented in his leadership. The country was united. As the opposition movement united further, the Shah grew desperate for support from the United States and his other Western allies. The British government not only abandoned the Shah, but now, through the BBC Radio, was helping Iranians get rid of him. All the messages from Ayatollah Khomeini to his followers were broadcast on BBC, Voice of America and Radio Israel.

Khomeini was exiled by the Shah to Iraq, and he sent messages to Iran, keeping contact with the people. As the people became more angry and frustrated with the Shah, Khomeini looked like Mandela. Saddam Hussein forced Ayatollah Khomeini out of Iraq as he became more powerful and appeared like a threat. Intellectuals around the world found Ayatollah Khomeini a safe refuge in Paris, where he established a powerful presence on the world stage.

n August 19, 1978 we woke up and heard the tragic news—a fire in the Rex Cinema captured the attention of all Iran—more than 400 people were burned to death in Abadan, in the South, where black gold ran through the veins of Iran. All the doors of the cinema had been locked from outside and the place was set on fire with no way for the people inside to escape. Four hundred innocent citizens were scorched. The opposition claimed that it was the regime's conspiracy to stop the movement. Evidence showed that the fire had been set by a radical, underground group that wanted to support the Revolution. They would use any means to shut down the Shah's government, including this terrorist action. A few months after the revolution, a court action revealed the perpetrators, and they were immediately executed, so no more information was ever released about their identities or affiliations.

Anyone who was ambivalent turned against the Shah and his SAVAK, who were blamed for this horrible disaster. Then Black Friday occurred on September 7, 1978, when the army opened fire on demonstrators and killed more innocents. My rebel soul was on fire. I had to fight or leave.

October, 1978 was the deadline for Khosro to commit to study at MIT. So we hurriedly made plans to leave. We finished building our house and made two apartments. We rented one and put all our belongings into the other. Mom moved into the new apartment and stayed there very close to Aki. I had the two boys and was pregnant.

In my heart I was prepared to leave Iran forever and try to bring Mom to the United States. I could see bloody days ahead in Iran. Even though our political friends advised us not to move, I wanted to leave. This opportunity was part of my dream—a bright road for us to travel.

First, Khosro and I discussed the scholarship with Mr. Bazargan, and he advised us to continue our lives, that education was the first priority to serve our country in the future. This made my heart even stronger. I asked if we could stop in Paris and see Ayatollah Khomeini. I believed in him, that he was trying to change the regime peacefully. The way he talked, all the tapes and papers promised peaceful change. That's why the Shah left the country peacefully. I thought everything will be in peace. I wanted to confirm this with Ayatollah Khomeini, even though I was just an insignificant individual.

Through Mr. Bazargan we received permission to see Ayatollah Khomeini in Paris on our way to the United States. Khosro and I traveled to Paris with Hooman, Arshia, and our nephew Ali who had just graduated from high school and was going to continue his education in the United States. Ali, Aki's son, didn't return to Iran for 17 years after that trip.

We stayed in a hotel near the Ayatollah's residence, Neauphle-le-Chateau for almost a week. The day after we arrived, we prepared to meet the most important religious leader of Iran. Ayatollah was now well known to the world, because every day international reporters were waiting at his residence door—with many French police protecting him. Through this chaos, we were welcomed privately because of Mr. Barzagan, to meet and pray with him in his tent by the apple tree. This was a huge honor.

We entered the garden, a small green slice of peace with a huge apple tree in the middle. The white, large tent had Iranian rugs covering the floor. Many Iranians brought their wealth and jewelry to show their love and support for Ayatollah Khomeini, and then served him as cooks and servants. I loved this garden, with the beautiful rain showers and then emerging sun. I sat in the corner of the garden by the flowers, and thought how the magic carpet had transported our family from chaos to this place. I thought this magic carpet would one day take democracy to Iran.

At noon, when *Azan* started, everyone made *vouzu* and prepared for the Ayatollah. He came in front of them and they prayed behind him. I smelled pure Islam there—peace, cleanness, and friendship.

After the large prayer meeting, they announced a small group of us to go in to his private chambers. I was the only woman in this group. I was wearing a small scarf on my head in respect, but Ayatollah's private aide asked me to have a larger scarf to cover. We were discussing this issue when Ayatollah Khomeini saw us. He pointed very authoritatively to finish this and let me in. He didn't look at anyone's face—he seemed very strong and powerful, like stone. I compared him to Bazargan, who was also one of the movement's leaders, but soft and approachable. They were both charismatic, but in different ways.

Inside, the sparse room looked like a mosque, with old carpets covering the floor. It was not fancy at all, but very warm and simple. Ayatollah Khomeini was sitting on a folded blanket on the floor by the wall. Two microphones were held in front of him, and we fifteen chosen kneeled facing this powerful symbol, called "the new Gandhi of the East" by the New York Times. The door was closed. I could see the reporters behind us.

Ayatollah Khomeini lectured, *"In the name of God, the most merciful, Iran is a peaceful country. Millions of people throughout the whole country began to peacefully march—men, women, children, young and old, demanding that they did not want the Shah any more. The people have a right to choose. The Shah must go. Human rights demand this. Victory is due to the unity of minds, unity of all religions and unity of scholars and students, unity of spiritual and political leaders. People of Iran, let us reach success through this unity of minds. Let us redefine our own destiny. God is with us."*

Everyone cheered and chanted, "God is the greatest, oh mighty Ayatollah."

Our expectations of the Ayatollah were so high. One of the Iranian student representatives got permission to speak to him, but when he came closer to the Ayatollah, he shook, cried, and forgot what he wanted to ask.

Peter Jennings, journalist from the United States, asked the Ayatollah, "Iran and the US are allies. What will you do when you go back to Iran and gain power?"

Ayatollah Khomeini sand, "We don't want to be enemies with any country. As long as we are independent, we will be friends with every country."

The communist's group representative asked, "What will you do with Communists in Iran?"

He answered, "Every group in Iran has the right to practice their own ideas as long as it is peaceful."

Someone else asked, "What about the other religions?"

Ayatollah said, "As long as there is no problem, as long as they are Iranians, then Christians, Jews and everyone are welcome—Iran is their country."

I raised my hand to see if I could ask a question, and Ayatollah nodded yes. My question was, 'What are you going to do about women's rights?' But Khosro, who was so ambivalent about leaving our country in this politically pregnant moment, asked me if he could speak, and didn't wait for my answer.

He immediately asked Ayatollah Khomeini, "I have a scholarship to go to study in America, but this is a very historical moment in Iran. Do you think I should go to MIT, or go back to Iran right now?"

In a low and strong voice, he said, "Education is very important. No problem for you to go and continue your education."

I had my answer too in this moment, and didn't insist on asking my own question. My heart was so at peace now that I had the approval that we were doing the right thing.

Another day we returned to Neauphle-le-Chateau-, just to see the crowds and witness the history of that moment. My children played and didn't know what they were really witnessing. Ali and Khosro prayed behind Ayatollah. And I prayed among other women behind the men. When we finished praying, we went back to the hotel, checked out and headed for the airport.

We sit in four seats across the middle of the Pan Am airplane, in the first row. The plane engine hums a restful lullaby as the plane crosses the Atlantic Ocean to our new life. Ali sits across the aisle watching the movie and reading a magazine. I wondered when Aki would see him again. I think of freedom, and taking my children to the free land of opportunity. I think Khosro's brain can bloom in our new land. My heart is celebrating.

In January of 1979, one week later, we arrived in Boston. It was blistering cold. 12 days later, Ayatollah Khomeini left Paris for Iran.

We went first to Khosro's sister's (Mehry's) house and stayed with them for three weeks. During this time, with their help, we rented an apartment in Brookline, furnished it simply and moved in. Khosro became very busy with his course work. I was 6 months pregnant and trying to prepare for the new baby. Hooman was registered in first grade in a wonderful open school where I could see him from outside through the windows. It was wonderful to watch him blossoming, so culturally different than Iran, where young children were taught to sit quietly and raise hands for permission to do anything. Here, the children were more alive and free.

Arshia was in pre-school. Every day I could stay with him for one hour because of the language barrier. It was hard for him to adjust to the new environment.

Ali my nephew left for Richmond College in Connecticut.

And I was anxiously waiting for my new baby to arrive.

The relationship between Iran and the United States was

still good, so Khosro's scholarship funding was solid. However, after four months the relationship between countries became shaky and Khosro started worrying about his tuition payments. We were living comfortably but not above our means, so we were OK financially.

However, every day there was news about Iran and the protesters were like a thorn in our sides, constantly poking us. This caused my baby to move too much in utero, and my doctor warned me not to watch the news or think about Iran. It was impossible not to think about my country, with my mother and sisters there, in chaos.

Khosro was obsessed with the news and even went with his brother-in-law to purchase a short wave radio so he could always hear the Iranian news.

I was in hell. My husband barely even realized that I was pregnant and paid no attention to my needs to prepare. My children needed more attention to adjust to a new environment with a new baby coming, and we all felt Mom's absence. All the time I was in America, I felt guilty of abandoning Mom—like I had left her behind the same way that she had left Ashi with my father. We missed our family and busy social life in Iran. Besides all of this, that was the coldest winter on record in Boston.

In Iran something new was happening every day as it headed toward Revolution.

When the reform changed to Revolution on February 11, 1979 our minds were in crisis.

Khosro was not focused on his work. He asked me to stay in the US to have the baby and he would go to Iran, and then return to the US. His sister and her husband offered for me to stay and they would take care of me. But it was like a huge storm was coming, and I was not willing to leave my husband. I had a flash back to the time that my mother helped my father escape from Iran. I would follow him anywhere. At the time, Iran Air airline had direct flights from New York to Tehran. Twenty-two days before Salman was born, I followed Khosro back to a crumbling Iran.

Salman was born in the same hospital that Hooman and Arshia were born, with the same doctor. He was the most beautiful, handsome baby I had ever seen—big black eyes and special ordered by God. Any parent knows that it is so amazing to see that every tiny cell and vessel is in exactly the right place, and Salman was perfect. The nine months of pregnancy were like nine hundred years of events, beginning during a monarchy and ending during the Republic, with travel to Paris and America and back to Iran. The environment was familiar, but everything had changed. After all the turmoil, this peaceful child emerged into the world.

Mom hugged him and said, "You are my ninth promised ruby!"

I got a nanny for him under my mother's supervision. I registered the two other boys in international school and became involved in social work that was desperately needed.

hen we returned to Iran, Bazargan was Provisional Prime Minister of Iran.

During the nine months under Bazargan's leadership, Iranians had a taste of freedom and democracy, the same as Mossadeq had shown. But the radical Islamists under Ayatollah Khomeini's leadership leaned toward an Islamic revolution over democratic reform and Bazargan resigned within a year, complaining that these radical clerics were undermining his government.

The Revolutionary Council was formed by Ayatolallah Khomeini in January 1979 to supervise the transition from monarchy to republic. The Revolutionary Council remained in power and was in conflict with the provisional government, which vigorously tried to reestablish the power of law. The Revolutionary organization grew like mushrooms everywhere in the country, with *komitehs* (vigilante groups) overtaking local mosques and sabotaging everything in the name of the revolution. They became involved in military conflicts, arrests, property confiscations, trials and the firing and hiring of government agents. They even intervened in foreign policy. People were confused and terrorized, and the country became very unstable.

With the lack of Ayatollah Khomeini's support, Prime Minister Bazargan was left helpless. Finally on November 6, when young Islamic revolutionary students overran the United States Embassy in Tehran and took 60 Americans hostage, Bazargan, along with his cabinet, resigned out of complete frustration. The country became an orphan again as in the time of the coup against Dr. Mossadeq.

Bazargan complained, "When you want to act as a revolutionary, you do not have rules. You act like a bulldozer. I am not a bulldozer. I want to bring democracy to Iran "step by step." But the revolutionary leaders harassed and opposed him.

He vehemently opposed the US hostage-taking and openly showed his disapproval. But his resignation was mostly because of revolutionary intervention in his governing of the country. Also, his hopes for liberal democracy vanished and he could no longer do the job he felt destined to accomplish.

Bazargan never gave up and continued to serve in the Iranian parliament for years. He led the freedom movement of Iran. He peacefully and vigorously opposed radical opponents. He continued writing books and was active until his death in early 1995. He and his party were under horrendous pressure. Most people in the party were imprisoned and some were tortured. Now, after years, the young generation of Iranians who were born after the revolution read his books and listened to his lectures, trying to find democracy and to reach for his dreams. He gave me a Qur'an as a gift, dated and signed by him. It was on the *sofreh* table at my son's wedding.

E ach day I come to the garden with baggage. Sometimes it is worries, sometimes pain, sometimes big questions and sometimes just little annoyances. The inhabitants of the garden know just what I need, and how to help me understand my situation. They help with kindness one day, and with searing soul-searching honesty the next. They make me a better person, and let me cast away those things that do not serve me well. They even hide those things that would cause me harm.

One year and four months after Salman was born, the Iran-Iraq War began in September of 1980. It started because Saddam Hussein thought it might be a good time to invade Iran, hungry to acquire Iran's wealth. He wanted Iraq to become the dominant Middle Eastern presence. Thinking that the chaos in Iran meant a weakened military, Iraq went on the offensive. As it turned out, Iran was able to repel Iraq within two years and then the brave young Iranians went on the offensive for the next six years. Millions of young Iranians stood up to Saddam Hussein, half a million lost their lives and another million were injured.

During the first year of the Iran-Iraq war, when the city of

Khoram-shar was destroyed by Saddam Hussein, many orphan refugee children were brought to Tehran by government agents. Foster homes were notoriously abusive at that time with most kids either ending up as beggars, in prison or dead. The war environment drew all of us together in a net of support for those who were harmed, particularly the children. Because the universities and private businesses were closed, everyone had time to contribute.

With the help of a dedicated group of friends, we adopted 9 orphan boys, aged 5 to 12 years old and housed them in a government-confiscated mansion so they would not end up in a foster home. We were intent on saving these kids; they had just lost their parents and were incredibly vulnerable. Instead of foster care, they were able to live in a large 6 bedroom house with a huge backyard and a pool.

We were only able to get this house with the help of Mr. Bazargan, backed by Ayatollah Khomeini, without whom it would have been impossible. Eraj, Ashi's son, volunteered to become the caretaker of the house, driving the children to school, taking them shopping or running errands.

I found two retired, educated, middle-aged ladies to work in the house as managers, each every other day. Six female college students took the role of mother and sister during the day, and six college boys assumed the role of father and big brother at night. They all worked as volunteers. Ashi, Aki and most of my friends volunteered too.

Every individual in the country contributed in some way. The villagers made and donated food for the hospital. They made clothing for the patients from their bed sheets. Khosro and I managed the house like parents, and we were provided volunteer money to continue. These kids went to the same private school where our children went, with the same education and clothing. We all became a huge family.

In June 1980, Ashi, my sister, was living in the village of Evin, which houses the notorious Evin prison where many political prisoners have been tortured and killed over the past 50 years. Evin is located on top of a hill toward the Alborz Mountain, surrounded by snake-like, tall walls, barbed wire across the hill and protected by many armed guards. We heard that the city was in chaos. A group of Mujahedin militia had begun fighting Ayatollah Khomeini's revolutionary government. They held spontaneous demonstrations across Iran where hundreds of thousands of young people came out to shout their anger at the government. In some parts of Tehran, including our village, violent armed demonstrations broke out. No one knew what was going to happen and a heightened level of anxiety surrounded us.

I became worried about all of our nine children, but especially Ashi's son, Eraj, who was working at an orphanage. Eraj was not involved in any political group; he was very busy taking care of the children. I kept thinking that Eraj was out in the chaos with the children, without friends to protect him on either side. The thought would not leave my head. I put Salman (two years old) and Arshia (seven years old) in my Peugeot and went out to find him. It was very dangerous to be out and about at this time. I stopped at Ashi's to see if she knew where Eraj was. He was with her and I was so happy that he had not gone out and was safe.

At this point, I had not remembered that I had a gun in my car trunk that made it dangerous for all of us. When my uncle left for Canada, he hid his gun at Ashi's house. Having a gun at that time was grounds for immediate execution. The week before this uprising, because the house was close to Evin and the gun made things dangerous for Ashi and her family, I took it and was going to dispose of it so none of us would be at risk. The opportunity had not surfaced to get rid of this dangerous object.

As Salman, Arshia and I headed back home I noticed that the area around the prison was full of young *Basiji* (a low-ranking revolutionary guard) who had recently become the street militia behind Ayatollah Khomeini's revolution. They were confronting the Mujahedin rebels and the atmosphere was very tense. I was scared to death once the gravity of the situation sank in. It was like I had put my hand directly into a bee hive, as I remembered the danger in the trunk.

The boys were sitting in the back seat, quarreling. As I reached the barricades at the top of the hill, a *Basiji* ordered me to stop and get out and open the trunk. They were inspecting every car for weapons, or for any declaration or manifest. As I came to a stop, my whole body started to shake and I was trying to get out of the car but was frozen with fear.

The soldier yelled, "Get out!"

At the same time, my sons became very scared and Salman started climbing over the seat to grab me. Arshia was trying to hold him. Salman, crying that he wanted to come with me, suddenly grabbed the stick shift, putting the car into neutral. I had one foot out of the car and one foot coming off of the clutch when the car started to roll down hill.

I could feel the weight of the car pulling away from my powerless hands and saw my children rolling away from me, screaming and crying; I was paralyzed with fear.

Suddenly, the teenage *Basiji* pulled me out of the way, pushed Salman back in, jumped into the car and pulled the emergency brake.

When the car stopped, he turned to me and yelled, "Mother, why are you coming out on this crazy, chaotic day? Don't you know what's going on?"

Salman was crying like crazy. He then hugged Salman to calm him, gave him a kiss and put him in my arms. I felt a little safer at that fleeting moment.

Then he said, "Today is a very dangerous day. Where is your home?"

I told him my address.

He said "You will be stopped every five blocks. The secret password is *Oghab* (Eagle). So you say that and go straight home. Don't come back out today."

I drove home terrified, sweating and crying. As soon as I saw my mom I handed the boys to her and I said, "Eagle," then passed out.

The whole country tasted freedom for nine months when Bazargan was prime minister. Mr. Barzagan had a huge impact on my life and on the life of my generation. In 1981, there was no active social life for young people—no cinema, no University—only the war. Without Mr. Barzagan I could not have done my work with orphans and young people. He made people available to me who trusted him, and therefore me. These people provided funding, and the doctors who helped us and others loved Mr. Barzagan. Because of his name, all the liberals were willing to help us.

One of my self-selected missions was managing young volunteers at the hospital. The University was closed after the Revolution, so anyone who graduated from high school had nothing to do. I arranged a program in five hospitals, Center of Volunteer Helpers, where doctors trained the volunteers in first aid and I taught them nursing. In one year we trained 500 aides and the organization eventually grew to 1,000 individuals. This training was triage preparation, especially for war. We held classes and practice drills. Everyone learned and worked free, day and night. The volunteers were educated and ready to help, full of energy, smart and quick learners.

We had cooperation from many government officials and religious groups—Christian, Zoroastrian and Jewish amongst them, because we never asked about the religion of our volunteers and accepted anyone who came in good faith. Many lives were saved as a result of our program.

One of the volunteers with two years of experience was working in a field hospital tent near the battlefield. He noticed a young soldier who had a very bad stomach ache, vomiting and not able to rest. The volunteer diagnosed acute appendicitis and didn't have any choice but to do surgery himself or let the man die. In the morning, the attending doctor found out that the surgery had been successfully completed. This volunteer had learned in two years what usually took six; he was praised by the doctor in writing. Later, when he left the country, this letter got him admission to study medicine at a university in Poland. The soldier said he owed his life to this volunteer.

My house was very close to one of the general hospitals where seriously injured fighters were brought. Streets became the battlefields between the Mujahedin- Khalgh Organization (MKO) and Ayatollah Khomeini's regime. Although during the revolution, the MKO was the most loyal group of Ayatollah Khomeini's followers, a year later they became brutal enemies, each seeking to rule the country. The revolutionary court ordered thousands of young MKO to be killed. On the other hand, the MKO engaged in constant terrorist activity, planting bombs to kill indiscriminately and using suicide bombers to kill many revolutionary agents and ministers. The country was in turmoil. They set afire and burned to death the Prime Minister after Bazargan and several other ministers in their offices—only their teeth remained. There was a lot of terrorist activity by the Mujadehen, who were also killing one another. Every time I heard a helicopter, I rushed to the hospital.

One day, about 10 AM they brought in a wounded *mullah* (clergyman), covered in his own blood. The MKO had attacked him in the street. He was a huge man, difficult to move from the helicopter to a stretcher and then to a bed. He was brought to the emergency room and all the doctors swarmed around.

He looked dead, but the doctors were still trying. Doctors and helpers were in two secret groups. The doctors who really believed in him were doing their best, but eventually realized he was dead. I saw two young interns, however, who, by their actions, I knew were against him. I saw with my own eyes that the man was dead, but these two continued to give CPR so hard that they broke his ribs, mocking: "We don't want you to die, we don't want you to die." They showed their anger to this dead body.

I said, "Leave him alone. He is dead."

But they ignored me, and when they were done, sneaked out of the room.

One religious worker came and put his finger into the Mullah's blood and then touched his own forehead, blessing the Mullah, "Oh, my dear martyr, your blood is my life. I commit my life to you."

I watched this scene in shock—blood, a dead body, and two contrasting actions by medical professionals. I felt weak and confused and near a nervous breakdown. I couldn't feel anything— it was like being stuck in mud within a nightmare, while an angry, hungry animal tries to grab you.

I couldn't stay in the hospital any more. I left the emergency room to start for home, to escape from my feelings. In the entry of the emergency room was a very young (18-19 year old) lady who was the Mullah's wife. She was asking if he was alive and asked me to tell her what happened to him. I hugged her, kissed the baby; I cried with her but was mute.

I went home and told my mother what happened and then cried with Mom like a baby. At night, on the television and radio news, they announced that this Mullah was Ghorayshi, a representative of Ayatollah Khomeini in the Navy.

I'm very proud of the work we did at that hospital, and the system we created. But it was the wrong time and the wrong place. No matter what we tried, it would have not been successful in a culture wracked by war. Two years after the Revolution, "liberal" became a very negative label. That's how they took away our orphan children, and kicked us out of the hospitals—first two hospitals, then the others.

Little by little, they took away our freedoms. I tried to follow the rules to protect the program, wearing a scarf over my head as a sign of respect, but I was told not to wear a scarf, only a chador. I know that two of our volunteers eventually went to Poland and became doctors, and some others left the country as well. I don't know what happened to those who stayed. As my freedoms disappeared, I became ready to leave this land that I loved. It would be three years more before I actually left.

In the summer of 1987, we decided to leave Iran. Salman was about 8 and we were paralyzed because he didn't have a green card. We went to Turkey to apply for Salman's green card; there was no American embassy in Iran after the hostage crisis. We took a bus from Turkey to Iran, because there were few flights available at that time. At the border checkpoint, two armed guards one 14 and one 16 years old, came to the bus to check if anyone had any magazines, cards, alcohol—any sign of western culture. They had a bag and collected whatever they wanted. It made me very angry and I felt trapped in the bus. A woman sitting near the front of the bus showed a Dr. Seuss book and asked if they wanted this as well as the fashion magazines.

I objected to that woman, and asked her "Do you know your rights? Why do you encourage them by offering even children's books?" I hollered at her that she had to provide the child an education. "Why don't you know your rights?"

Then the guard said, "Oh, look how she's talking now? When we come to search everyone should obey us and they should show us everything. If we say to hand it over, then they should do it! Don't you know this?"

The boys remember that I was arguing with the guards, saying that I knew what Islam was and that their way was not the way my mother had taught me to practice, to accept all people and beliefs.

I was wearing a chador, but to be comfortable in the bus I had taken off my socks. It was late and we had been travelling all night so my *hijab* wasn't complete.

The young revolutionary guard ordered everyone off the bus. They didn't let me put my socks on, but pulled me out of the bus and took me to their commander in the checkpoint office.

Khosro anxiously followed me, saying, "My wife was sleeping. She is a very angry person. She doesn't feel good." He made excuses for me so they would think I wasn't normal.

Arshia and Salman had followed too. They were behind the open door of the building, watching me from the window. The soldiers didn't let the boys in.

In the *Komiteh* (revolutionary office), the older guard explained to the boss, "This woman was nude in the bus under her chador. When we were taking the forbidden things to follow the Islamic rule, she interrupted us. She made chaos and fun of the revolution's rules in the bus."

My children were pressing their faces against the window, saying "No, no, no, she wasn't nude. They are lying."

Then the boss said, "Oh, I see she has no socks under her chador. I can believe you, that's a sign that she was nude."

I started to object, "Why should I be nude in the bus? I was with my husband! I took my socks off because we are going to Tehran and it is almost 10 hours drive and I just wanted to be comfortable. Then the guards wouldn't let me put my socks back on before they took me out of the bus and brought me to you."

Khosro apologized deeply, "Oh, dear brother, please forgive her. She's not supposed to take her socks off."

I screamed at the boss, "Are you sitting there in the place of the prophet Mohammed judging me? You see me nude when I don't have my socks on? I don't believe in this Islam that you are imposing, because I am a Muslim the way my mother raised me— not this Islam."

He told the two guards, "Shut her mouth up. She talks too much! Take her out back. She has a long tongue. How dare you object to me like that? Do you know I can execute you right here behind this door? Or I could cut your tongue so you can't talk back any more. I'll make you mute! How dare you make fun of the revolution!"

Khosro was agitated, and my sons were pushing their faces into the glass windows. I could see them saying, "No, no, no!"

Then the boss left angrily and went into the back. The younger soldier, about Hooman's age, came to me and offered me water. He whispered in my ear, "Don't talk back. I am going to talk to him. Don't talk back any more."

So I accepted the water. I wasn't scared at all. I was ready to die that night. I didn't want to live with such humiliation and domineering force any longer. But when I looked at my children's faces, I felt very guilty that I wasn't able to control myself. And I was furious at my husband that he didn't fight them like me. But he was wise enough not to put us in more danger.

A few minutes later, the boss arrived with two guards, and said, "This younger boy told a different story about the bus to me. He refuted the older one's story. I'm going out to ask the people what really happened in the bus. Then I will decide what to do with you tonight."

He went out, investigated and then he came back.

He started talking Turkish to me. "Are you from Azerbaijan?"

I said, "Yes."

He said, "Azeri women have more respect for men than you showed us. You have to obey your husband. He is a gentleman—calm and apologizing all the time. But you're a rebel! If you weren't Azeri, I would kill you tonight. But I forgive you, because you are an Azeri woman, and people in the bus didn't see you nude or doing anything suspicious."

Then Khosro said, "Please explain what you are saying in Turkish." He thought they were going to kill me.

Khosro asked me to translate. I told him in Farsi, "He said I am a beautiful wife for you because I am Azeri."

The guy hollered at the two guards, "Take her out of here before I kill her! She is very crazy!"

We all went out. My children embraced me like I was born again.

People from the bus were very angry at me. "Couldn't you just shut up and sit in the bus? We've been here for two hours because of you!"

Even some said, "What did you have to hide that you were so nervous?"

But I had nothing to hide—I was defending my rights, and theirs.

When we returned to the bus, I promised myself that I was leaving this country with my children. My mom once told me to "Shut up and run." I didn't learn from her advice, and now I nearly lost my life because of it.

In 1985, in the middle of the Iran-Iraq war, I left Iran with Arshia, my middle son, to gain our green cards again. After two years of hell, our family finally joined together in Connecticut to begin a new chapter of our lives, in 1987.

I became a citizen of the United States and then went to Turkey in 1994 to get Mom. We went out shopping to buy candlesticks and gifts for the children. The night before our flight to JFK in New York, I noticed Mom was passed out on the hotel bed for a short time. I tried to move her but she wasn't conscious. I gave her CPR and a neighbor in the hotel was a pharmacist who gave her an adrenaline injection. All night I read the Qur'an into her ear, telling her to be strong, she was going to see Hooman, Arshia, and Salman. When the Turkish mosque announced *Azan* at sunrise, she miraculously opened her eyes and asked me where we were.

She said, "Am I in America?"

I said, "No, we're on the way."

She asked for her prayer rug and prayed as usual.

I didn't take her to the hospital, or she would have lost her green card. I prayed and read the Qur'an the whole night, begging God to help me take her to America to see my children.

She was too weak to walk, so I took her in a wheel chair to the airport. She fought her weakness and she tried to help me as much as she could. She wiggled her hands and feet and massaged her body to keep warm. She prayed constantly, her lips moving and whispering. She sometimes called Parviz and her father's name, as though they were traveling with us and protecting her.

I cried, prayed and willed ourselves across the ocean until we landed at JFK in New York. We were strong together, as we disembarked the airplane. Khosro and the children all hugged Mom. I kissed her and we went home to Connecticut.

Mom felt well right away. She recognized everybody, except that she was looking for baby Salman instead of the 10 year old that he had become.

Four days later she had the same symptoms, so we took her to the hospital where we learned that she had a heart attack. But she recovered and she lived with us for five more years.

She enjoyed most of these days more than us. She had no language barrier because she could read gestures and loved everyone unconditionally. She loved all of Salman's friends and they loved her. Her relationship with Aaron, Salman's best friend and Susan's (my co-author's) son, was tender and very close. Even though they did not speak the same language, they shared a language of the heart that was deeper than words and they took care of each other. She gave a grandmother's love to him.

Mom never gave up. Her father comforted her with a gift of 9 rubies when her only son, Parviz, passed away in Ardebil at age 5.

He said, "You are supposed to have 10 sons. He took one away, but he's going to give you 9 back. You're going to have 9 grandsons, each as precious as one of these rubies."

He told her, "Don't give up; Be a good Muslim and understand that God is the one in control, not you. Don't waste your time trying to control an issue. I am appealing to God to take care of these children, and after God I am asking you to sacrifice your life for them. I hope you can raise them with the things that I am leaving behind for you. If you stay strong and don't lose your faith, I know Parviz and I will meet you when you die. Life is not easy."

Postlude

Aki was a devoted mother to her three children, but she didn't stop helping us. She worked to take care of our other sister, Ashi, who needed a lot of help and to take care of Mom when she needed her. She is now the best aunt to her nephews that anyone could wish for, and they love her unconditionally.

After she gave birth to her first child at age 16, Aki started to study by herself from 7th grade. She finished high school without going to school. She studied and took a test. At 24 she took the entrance exam for the university. It was very difficult, but she passed with a great score and honor. When she went to register for university, they said she was over age. That was the second rejection, and it really wounded Aki. But this unjust rejection didn't stop her from continuing her education. She became self- educated in psychology and social work. In 1970, she was hired as a social worker in Shohada General Hospital (before called Reza Pahlavi) after passing the hospital's examination. She was very helpful and understanding in this environment, especially during the hard time of war.

Later on she worked 15 years with a psychologist who graduated from Harvard, and she was great at that as well, helping a lot of people. That doctor from Harvard said if it wasn't for lack of a diploma she could be in charge of the clinic floor where she worked. Emotionally, the doctor helped Aki to find out a lot about herself. She eventually sent her only son to the United States for a higher education. She lives in Iran with her husband, two daughters and four grandchildren, and has a peaceful, lovely life. Her children are surprised that at her age she has learned so much about the computer on her own, and now is teaching her grandchildren!

Ashi lived with Yadi for ten years. During these years Ashi was raising two boys and studied hard until she became a practical nurse and served her country the best way she could during the war. She is the hero in our family, a nurse. At age 24, she started to work in Albourz Hospital in Tehran. She got divorced from Yadi, now 64 years old. Yadi was a good father and helped Ashi raise the two boys, Eraj and Touraj.

One year later Ashi married a man her own age. Through this marriage she gave birth to three more boys. She provided five of Grandfather's promised rubies.

She is one of the most spiritual, devoted mothers ever. She is the center of prayer for all of us. Four of her boys are taking care of her like a queen.

When I finished four years of nursing school I started to work in three hospitals simultaneously in 3 shifts. I worked one year and was able to get an apartment and fixed it for Mom. She came to live with me there and left her job. I found a wonderful husband and had three sons. I never lived without my mother, and Khosro replaced her lost son. I continued my education and became a counselor in adolescent crisis. My family settled in the Northeast United States. I now have an international family with two wonderful Danish and American daughter-in-laws, and waiting for a third one, and one amazing granddaughter named Tina, my own special ruby.

I don't hate Rasoul any more, and have a little place in my

heart for my father and his political way in the world.

Mom stayed in the United States for five years with us. She enjoyed Sue's and Cindy's family like her own. In some way, she saw Parviz in Aaron, Sue's son. Each time I mentioned his name she said, "You mean my Parviz." She loved Aaron dearly. She never felt foreign in the United States and everyone she met loved her. She loved President Clinton, and called him the "King of the United States" and prayed for him every night. She followed every moment of OJ Simpson's trial and from the beginning she said, "I know he did it."

Mom had no plans to travel, but strangely, she woke up one morning in February of 1999, and asked me to take her back to Iran. With her heart condition doctors advised her not to travel but she insisted that it was time for her to go. My friends arranged a beautiful goodbye party for her with lots of love and gifts.

On February 17, 1999, I took her back to Iran. When we arrived, Ashi and Aki and their children had a beautiful welcome party for her, and surprised us by inviting the whole family. Mom had a gift for each of them. That night many videos were shown of the times she had missed when she was not in Iran, like wedding parties or birthdays. She was extremely happy and told everybody, "I feel like a queen. I think it is my wedding tonight." She left the party before other guests by saying, "Goodbye, everybody. I love you all." And she threw a kiss.

She died in her daughters' arms 48 hours after. She saw her 9 rubies and then she went to God. When I think about those last hours of my mother's life, I think only God could have managed such a perfect ending for her.

Today I have two countries that I love, one in which I was

born and one in which I made my new life. I always pray for a peaceful relationship to grow between them—Iran with more than 3,000 years heritage, and America with freedom and democracy, however flawed.

My soul wanders between the two countries. I have dear friends here and there. I often feel tormented, living in both worlds with one body and a divided soul. However heart-wrenching, I am privileged to have experienced such profound depth and insight during my life....it has provided me with strength... and made me true to the fire of my soul.

THE END

Nine Rubies – Reading Group Guide

Mahru and Sue started out as strangers. Mahru says that she remembers Sue preparing a group of parents for some event where we sang for our children – perhaps graduation from 6th Grade – dancing all around. She thought Sue was great, and full of what she loved. "On that day with Sue's dance and music, my mind traveled to the time when her mom was dancing to Turkish music, and I was so happy that I cried."

Sue remembers going to Mahru's home to pick Aaron up after a play date, and marveling at the woodland retreat, Persian carpets, and Mahru's aesthetic sense. "It smelled divine, and Mahru's mom quietly sat and smiled. Mahru was warm, welcoming, and wonderful."

When these two women began to converse, Mahru was very sad. Her background in oral history helped Sue find a way to listen, and each story was revealed to Mahru as she spoke it. Mahru's storytelling was riveting from the start. The most painful memories were the last to emerge, coaxed out of dark corners of Mahru's memory by the growing safety of the relationship. The interaction was never designed to create a book, but rather to help a friend find comfort by opening those doors that were slammed shut and barricaded from the inside.

Mahru and Sue both loved to nature, sunlight, the moon, gardens and flowers, deer and birds, laughter, entertaining - but especially shared the solitude and peace of the outdoors. (They both are good cooks, but share a conditional relationship with cooking – they cook well for those they love, but don't love to cook!) They walked and drank in nature as a release from the intensity of stories told and collected, and became sisters through shared histories and experiences. They also loved words, and how poetic prose has an embedded artistry that allows words to move beyond the literal, and represent the ethereal feelings and impressions that cannot be described in mere words alone. Each story started out feeling perfectly normal, even maybe a little dull, and all of a sudden slid into an out-of-the-ordinary experience – the kind that changes a life forever.

Prejudice was also a shared experience between the two women. They both grew up poor, but feeling special – feeling somehow foreign in their homes. They both felt insecure about where they fit in the world. And they both grew up in families where intellect and art were valued, but where those values were kept at arm's length as something to strive for, but perhaps never to achieve or embrace.

The juxtaposition of the peaceful garden, the jarring personal experiences, and the historical context of huge change that signaled the onset of the contemporary Iranian/American struggle acted as three huge threads to be woven together, each becoming a metaphor for the other, as <u>Nine Rubies</u> was knit together. How interesting to live in this world of words and metaphor, while also living full lives in which our sons matured, learned, and became men.

DISCUSSION

1. Khalil Gibran advises at the beginning of the book, "The deeper that sorrow carves into your being, the more joy you can contain." Think of examples in your experience of people who have been hurt deeply, and yet have through resilience ended up more joyful or stronger than they were? Has there a sad experience in your life that made you stronger? What are the common experiences that most of us share that are sorrowful?

2. Iranians consider themselves Persian; Persia is the old name for Iran. Within Persia/Iran, there are many religions and cultural groups. How is this similar to the country where you live, and how is it different? Discuss anything you learned in the book about how people deal with differences within their community and/or more broadly.

3. This story involves "coming of age" of young girls. Compare the experiences of the women in this book, and what falls into the realm of normal, and what is considered abusive. Are there situations that you know about where young girls are treated in the ways these girls were brought up?

4. Music, dance and storytelling were very important to Mahru as she grew, and her mother made sure her children had cultural and artistic experiences at a young age. Discuss your mother's role in your life in regard to your cultural and artistic sensibilities.

5. Discuss whether the mother made good decisions. Could she have done anything differently? What was within her control? What was

not within her control? What biases and opinions helped or hurt her as she made decisions? What might have happened if she decided to marry Dr. Vaziri, either earlier or later in her life? What do you think you would have done? Have you ever had to make decisions when there seem to be only bad choices?

6. The '60s were a time of increasing popular culture around the world. Discuss how Mahru's experiences and with her friends were similar and different from those you experienced or have heard about the '60s. Were you surprised to hear about the influence of Elvis, the Beatles, and jeans in Iran? What influences of Western culture do you think Iranian girls today look toward as popular culture?

7. The experience with Behrooz is not uncommon among immigrants or individuals escaping from one place to another at times of crisis. Many, many families across the globe have been separated or destroyed by political situations. What was your feeling when you learned about Mahru and Behrooz's relationship? Have you ever had, or do you know about, people who are attracted to one another but should not be together for one reason or another? Is there any lesson to be learned from how Mahru dealt with this situation?

8. There are times in this story where impulse control would have changed the outcome. Discuss the moments when the characters acted impulsively, and whether you would have done the same thing or not. Do you think the actions were justified? What were the ramifications for those around the individual who acted impulsively? Have you ever acted impulsively to defend something you believe in? Have you ever squelched the impulse to act? Was it the right decision?

9. There are many metaphors in this story, where something comes to represent a feeling, an individual, or a situation. Discuss the role of the garden in the story, and what it represents for the characters, and for the story itself.

10. Discuss the role of the men in the book, and how they are represented. What resonates with your personal experiences, and where do you experience contrasts to the characteristics experienced in the text?

11. What does this book lead you to wonder about, and what actions does it inspire you to take in your life? What is the enduring result, if any, of your experience with this story? What is your action plan?

12. The authors formed a friendship over several years, taking a journey through which trust was built. Discuss the characteristics of a friendship that reaches a level where someone can feel safe to share stories such as these. What are the risks one takes when sharing such personal experiences? What would you do if someone shared a personal story with you? What are a listener's responsibilties?

For additional questions and discussion, go to
www.ninerubiesthebook.com.

9. There are many metaphors in this story, where something comes to represent a feeling, an individual, or a situation. Discuss the role of the garden in the story, and what it represents for the characters, and for the story itself.

10. Discuss the role of the men in the book, and how they are represented. What resonates with your personal experiences, and where do you experience contrasts to the characteristics experienced in the text?

11. What does this book lead you to wonder about, and what actions does it inspire you to take in your life? What is the enduring result, if any, of your experience with this story? What is your action plan?

12. The authors formed a friendship over several years, taking a journey through which trust was built. Discuss the characteristics of a friendship that reaches a level where someone can feel safe to share stories such as these. What are the risks one takes when sharing such personal experiences? What would you do if someone shared a personal story with you? What are a listener's responsibilties?

For additional questions and discussion, go to
www.ninerubiesthebook.com.

CPSIA information can be obtained at www.ICGtesting.com
Printed in the USA
LVOW112149120612

285865LV00004B/1/P